DEAR LOVER

Important Caution
Please Read This

Although anyone may find the practices, disciplines, and understandings in this book to be useful, it is made available with the understanding that neither the author nor the publisher is engaged in presenting specific medical, psychological, emotional, sexual, or spiritual advice. Nor is anything in this book intended to be a diagnosis, prescription, recommendation, or cure for any specific kind of medical, psychological, emotional, sexual, or spiritual problem. Each person has unique needs and this book cannot take these individual differences into account. Each person should engage in a program of treatment, prevention, cure, or general health only in consultation with a licensed, qualified physician, therapist, or other competent professional. Any person suffering from venereal disease or any local illness of his or her sexual organs or prostate gland should consult a medical doctor and a qualified instructor of sexual yoga before practicing the sexual methods described in this book.

Sounds True, Inc., Boulder CO 80306

Published 2005
Printed in Canada

ISBN 978-1-59179-260-4

Library of Congress Control Number: 2004117957

Cover photo © Pure – nonstock.com

10 9

DEAR LOVER

a woman's guide to men, sex, and love's deepest bliss

DAVID DEIDA

Table of Contents

Foreword by Marianne Williamson

Like many women I know, romantic love is either all I want to talk about, or the last thing I want to talk about, depending on the hour. When I'm in the mood to discuss it, it seems huge and important. When I'm not in the mood, it seems almost neurotic. One thing remains constant, however, regardless of how I view it: romantic love is a mystery.

While it's many things to many people, rarely is romance the caricature we see portrayed in consumer advertising. It is grittier and more potentially painful than a picture of lovers walking the beach would indicate. Romance is more than a melodramatic container for alternating energies of bliss and despair, but to say what it is not is not the same thing as saying what it is. And that, perhaps, is because what it is, is changing. Like everything else, it is finding its spiritual element. It is rising up to meet us at the level of who we really are.

Viewed spiritually, romance is, in its divine essence, a temple space. It is one of God's laboratories, a mode of spiritual transformation. It is, when held this way, a sacred opportunity for souls to jump past the confines of the narrow self, to take quantum leaps forward into new and uncharted emotional possibilities. There love corners us, putting a mirror up to our faces and demanding that we surrender: surrender the hurt, surrender the past, surrender the walls, surrender the blame, surrender the defenses, surrender the limits, surrender the fear...

Love is not a game for sissies.

Most women I know are convinced by now, that spiritual surrender is the portal to love. Yet knowing that only goes so far. "Surrender?" we say. "I get the concept—but show me how!" For it's not so easy to surrender to love, when Daddy wasn't really there. It's not so easy to surrender to love, when someone we trusted abandoned or betrayed us. And it's not so easy to surrender to love when the last relationship left us psychically bleeding for months or even years.

It can take a lot of emotional effort to learn how to open the heart when the experience of life has shut it down. What we had thought were merely temporary protective mechanisms can become hardened over the years into entrenched defensive patterns. And we so grieve the ease and freedom of love.

We remember what we lost when we are reading Shakespeare's sonnets. We remember what we long for, reading Elizabeth Barrett Browning's poems to her beloved Robert. We remember the miracle we most want in our lives, listening to our favorite music late at night, the heart yearning purely and exquisitely for what it most deeply wants.

That yearning itself is a prayer for the kind of wisdom that David Deida imparts. He is one of our new romantic shamans. Deida is outrageous and blunt and sometimes over the top. He howls as well as whispers; he confronts as well as comforts. The fire he carries can either burn or enlighten, depending on our use of it. But if his fiery gift is a gift for you, then I think that you will know it. You will feel the parts of you that need his message, and you will feel yourself eager to receive it. Your mind and heart will respond to the idea that we can learn how to love in a more meaningful way, delivering us from the patterns of pain that have plagued our journey so far.

The journey to the heart of God is always the key to our deliverance, regardless of the source of our pain. But seeing how to apply that understanding is not always so easy when the pain strikes, the phone does not ring, the agreement is broken, or the hope is shattered. I am a little bit closer to my own love because I have listened to Deida and read this book. My heart is freer; may yours be too.

Now sit back on a comfortable pillow. Dim the lights, except around this book. Say a prayer perhaps, and ask for the truth that lies beyond the veil. Pray to learn about men what you need to learn, that you might learn to love them as you most long to do.

And then listen with me to the wizard of romance. He speaks to us of a long lost promise. He speaks of truth. He speaks of love.

Introduction

Dear Reader,

I offer the following chapters to you as if you were my lover. Although you may be single or married, I offer these words to you as I would to my beloved. We may never meet, but I want to give you the opportunity to feel your heart through mine.

For years, I have taught workshops around the world, opening with women and men while they share their deepest heart's desires. It seems we often come to know ourselves most deeply through the heart of someone who loves us, who is willing to open and see us as we truly are, who is willing to listen and feel our heart's yearning.

To give and receive love fully—this is our heart's true desire, yours and mine. The yearning you feel in your heart is the same yearning that everyone feels. By feeling your heart's yearning through mine, I hope you will come to know yourself more deeply through the many hearts that have opened together in trust and allowed these words to emerge.

All hearts want to open to God, or the boundless flow of divine love. You may or may not be a religious person, and still your heart yearns to open without bounds, to be seen and to be offered without limits. This is what I mean by "open to God"—to open and feel everything and everyone's heart as a divine expression of love.

Sexuality is also a divine expression of love—or at least it could be. As I would offer my heart to my lover, the following chapters are offered to you so your heart may open to God, whether you are alone or in relationship, whether you are making tea or making love. My hope is that by feeling your heart through these words, you will come to know more deeply how divine love yearns to open through everyone's heart.

And so, recognizing that our hearts flow open with the same love, the following chapters are offered to you as if you were my dear lover.

David Deida

1.

You Are Love

e⁀

Dear lover, when I look into your eyes, I feel your heart's yearning. Nothing is more beautiful to me than your love. I want to drink your love and dive into your heart and take you open to God. But I need to feel you wanting me to enter you. I want to feel you let down your guard in trust, just a little bit, so I can feel your heart's invitation. Please, open so I may claim your heart.

When you feel deep into your heart, you feel love. Most deeply, you *are* love.

This love shines as light, and so you want to be truly *seen*.

This light flows as energy, and so you want to *offer* yourself completely.

Your heart wants to give and receive love fully. This is your heart's deepest desire.

Love is openness. This same openness yearns at everybody's heart. You are this love. You are alive as love, and your entire body yearns to live open as love. Your heart wants nothing more than to live open as love, to give yourself totally as love—and to be seen as the love that you are. You long to be *claimed*, taken open, surrendered bliss- fully, so that every moment of your life is ablaze as the light of love's passion, an offering of your heart's devotion, and adoration of love's radiant blessing.

In an effort to create safety and self-reliance in your life and relation- ships, you may have built walls around your heart and accumulated tension in your body. Although sometimes these walls of protection are useful, they can, over time, act like shells of fear that block your true love. These shells can keep in the love you want to offer fully and keep out the love that your heart yearns to receive deeply.

The secret to unfolding your heart's deepest bliss is to give and receive love fully, with or without a man. Instead of depending on a man, and instead of protecting your heart behind walls of accumulated disap- pointment, you can learn to open your body as if it were a big heart, vulnerable and full of love's radiant life-force. And it is this disposition of openhearted radiance that will gift the world as well as attract and keep a man capable of actually meeting your heart's deepest desire.

Right now, is your breath textured as love—are you inhaling and exhal- ing with the same open pleasure you would if your lover's body were pressing against yours in delicate merger—or is your breath tense with fearful thoughts of self-survival as well as an emotional sense of separation, desperation, or loneliness?

Whether you are alone or in relationship, your spiritual and sexual bliss require a daily allotment of whole-body pleasure and deep heart offering, or else your joy will shrivel like an unwatered plant.

2.

Chocolate
Love

~

I love to watch you move. Your body is so open, I want to embrace you and hold your heart against mine. When I see you eat chocolate or your favorite foods, I am amazed at how your body responds by opening and softening in pleasure as if love were moving through you. You often quiver and make sounds of such delight. I wonder why you would choose to live any other way but this open to love. I know you can't always be eating delicious delicacies, but I wonder how you would live if you were breathing and feeling divine ambrosia moving through your body right now.

You can surrender open and allow the full love-energy of your heart to flow through your body all day. You can learn to open so your heart's love can flow fully through your *entire* body. Then, your true heart's light can shine through your eyes and smile. Love's energy can flow through the way you move. Love's openness can breathe you. Others can see who you truly are. They can feel your deepest gifts. You are love, flowing with love, bright as love.

By learning to open to love's fullest pleasure, your heart can express your deepest gifts through your body all day, and you will naturally attract and keep a lover whose deep heart is capable of meeting yours.

Imagine that you sit down with a bowl of your favorite treat—double chocolate ice cream with pecans. The first spoonful enters your mouth. Chocolate permeates your tongue like a delicious wave of fullness. Your eyes close and you smile. Mmmm! Love's blissful openness spreads through your whole body. You breathe fully, inhaling the chocolate aroma, the soft ice cream melting in your mouth. Even your toes and fingers may begin moving with pleasure as you swallow chocolate fullness.

If you wanted to allow pleasurable energy to move through your body even more, if you wanted to open every part of your body to overflow with love's fullness, then you could put down the bowl and stand up. You could give yourself over to chocolate madness, allowing your body to open and dance in chocolaty pleasure, writhing and swaying, moaning in yummy surrender.

You can allow energy to move through your entire body like electricity, opening you to a deeper flow of pleasure. You may even choose to allow sexual energy to move through you, touching your legs with your hands, writhing your hips in a voluptuous dance. You've gone way beyond the pleasure of chocolate now, feeling the flow of deeper passion and yearning in your body and heart.

Perhaps you lie on the couch and touch yourself between your thighs, wet with desire, full of wildness. Your tongue licks your lips wanting more, wanting more fullness to take in, more fullness to receive through your mouth, your belly, between your legs. Your legs open and close like butterfly wings as you touch yourself, surrendering open in the flow of energy and desire.

And then you may feel your heart, aching to be seen, wanting to be entered by love. More deeply than pleasure and energy, you want love. And not just your mother's love. Most likely, you want to feel a passionate man of true heart-integrity loving you deeply. You want him to see who you really are and desire you, feeling into your deepest heart. You want his tender force of love-desire to enter you deeply, opening your heart's secret core and unfolding your divine essence of love.

Although you may be reluctant to trust your own love's yearning, your deepest heart waits to be loved so fully that you are opened more than you are willing to open by yourself, blissfully forced open by love's deepest claim, revealed open and held in love's gentle command.

At times, you yearn for *him*. Not necessarily a specific man, but a force of masculine love, seeing who you really are, entering you, gently forcing you open with pleasure, massive love, insisting, persisting, unyielding in desire for you, loving deeper into you and opening you, not stopping. You are filled by his love, taken open by his claim. Breathing more and more deeply, your body undulates, pressed open by his weight, filled by love's enormity.

Your edges melt. Your boundaries dissolve. Your body opens outward, love radiating from your heart as an unkept offering. You cry as your resistance is melted in love's fullness, pleasure forcing your body more open. Your face moist, your thighs wet, your belly heaving, you surrender open, as wide as all. No boundaries. All love, all openness, all fullness.

After opening so fully, you feel permeated by love's ever-present touch for the rest of the day. As you walk through your home or carry on with your work, your hips move as a flower opens. Your belly is full of sky and stars. Your heart is offered ocean-deep. Washing the dishes or phoning your friends, love spills from your every gesture, blessing all with the abundant radiance of your heart.

Chocolate or a good man can instigate your heart's surrender, but full-bodied pleasure and overflowing love—opening until you are exposed fully to God as love's bliss— is the only way to live true to your deepest desire, with or without a trustable lover or a tasty dessert.

3.

Yearning Is the
Key to Love

Your yearning for love is so powerful that I can feel your heart all the time. When you openly love me I can feel your heart, but I can also feel your heart's yearning when you are angry or sad. To me, your heart is always calling, even though sometimes I am unable to open with you because your emotions divert me. I may be afraid or distracted and you may be upset, but still I feel your heart's yearning. And I need to feel your heart. Your yearning draws me back into love's depth. Your yearning is my invitation into your heart.

Feel deep into your heart. Feel your tremendous yearning. Although you may sometimes reduce this deep yearning to shallow neediness—the need to be loved by a man or by yourself—actually this deep yearning *is* the openness of love. This yearning is the hole through which the divine love that lives open as the universe can be felt to emerge. Your boundless depth of love comes to light through this hole of yearning when you trust open as love's ache.

Deep heart yearning is not a problem to be solved, but a divine pull to open as devotional surrender, as wide as all, now. With or without a man, whether or not you feel worthy, you can offer your heart's openness through your yearning, right now, as you are.

This capacity to offer your open love is indestructible. No amount of rejection or betrayal can destroy this offering of love. You may still at times feel hurt, tortured, and mangled in the fearful denial of love that your man, friends, and family may inflict on you, but their denial need not instigate yours. In the face of rejection and unlove, you can continue to open as the full strength of your heart's yearning and devotional surrender, opening in spite of the hurt that your unprotected heart feels, opening in the midst of emotional upheaval, yours and others'.

Devotional love is unstoppable, if you will only offer yourself wide open in the midst of suffering. If you are in a relationship, and your man is being a jerk, you may offer love's yearning as a strong demand: "I love you, and I won't tolerate less than your fullest consciousness." You may yell at him, and your rage may shake the house, but your heart need not close in the midst of love's fury.

When you love somebody fully, your heart's wrath may naturally be evoked in response to their repeated refusal to offer their deepest gifts. Anger may be your deepest expression of love in a moment of being frustrated by your lover's chosen limits and numb denial.

In any case, whether you are angry or hurt—beneath and through *all* emotions—your love yearns. This indestructible love is the same love, or openness, that yearns at the heart of all beings. Even when you are tense or upset, you can practice surrendering your body and heart to be breathed open by this love that yearns in everybody's heart.

4.

The Gift of
Making Love

⌇

I open my body to love's flow the most when
I open with you sexually. Usually my body is
something I use—to work, to play, to get things
done. But when I feel your body opening to mine,
my body remembers love. Your sexual surrender
awakens me to a depth of love I rarely feel in
my body during any other time of the day. And
through <u>entering your heart and body with
mine in love's deepest bliss, I open together with
you to God</u>. Your pleasure of surrender blesses
my life and opens me in ways that feel new and
deeper every time we make love.

Your yearning attracts and inspires love. If you allow your deepest yearning to show through your entire body, you will attract and inspire a deep man. How would a deep man love you?

A deep man is acutely aware of death: his, yours, and everyone's. Because he is always practicing to let go of everything, his consciousness is free, and he can be totally present with you. He can truly see you, he can feel your deepest heart, and he can enter you completely. As if this were his last moment on earth with you, he is unafraid to lose everything in his full offering of love.

Imagine that such a man were making love with you. He can feel his deepest purpose. Right now, he wants to open with you in utter heart surrender. From his deepest heart, he wants to enter you and take you open in love beyond all bounds. He gazes into your eyes and breathes with you, entering your heart fully, inhabiting your deepest heart's yearning.

You can feel his presence opening you. His gaze penetrates into your heart's hidden love. He offers you a concentrated invasion of divine presence. Love's masculine presence enters you more deeply than you could open yourself.

You can still feel your man's gaze holding your heart open deep, while his hand touches your body, gently, tenderly. Your breath deepens, and you can feel your man breathing with you. No part of you escapes his awareness. If your toe moves, he feels it. As your body shifts, he shifts with you, never letting you escape the claim of his full presence. He knows where to touch you and how to love you as he listens to your body's ripples and heart's response.

You don't hold back. His tender touch and forceful gaze open your desire. You move to kiss him. He receives your kiss, but doesn't stir. He smiles. You can feel him teasing you. You kiss him again, more forcefully. Again, he smiles and remains lovingly indifferent, although his gaze and touch continue to inhabit your every motion.

You can't stand it anymore and you roll on top of him, yearning for his deeper entrance, longing to be taken by this man who feels you so deeply and unerringly. Your soft bellies breathe together as you gaze into each other's eyes. His eyes seem endless, and yet they also seem steely, intense, laser-like. And suddenly he pounces—you are on your back and he pins you beneath him.

You gasp as his legs open yours. But he waits. He breathes with you. You can feel his hardness and the force of his belly against your belly, breathing with you, opening you with his full breath, in and out of your heart, his belly pressing into yours, his feet pinning yours to the bed, his hands holding your wrists. He gazes into your eyes.

He continues feeling his own death, your death, everyone's death. He feels the preciousness of this moment, the delicate love at everyone's heart, the gift of being born in the form of a man and woman. He feels love's open depth living through him, living through both of your forms. He connects with your heart through his gaze, his belly pressing into you, breathing you. He is so present with you that you can't help but open more deeply, surrendering beneath the weight of his heavy love, opening your legs to draw him in.

He looks down at your breasts. He smiles. You can feel him adoring your feminine form. He kisses your breasts, gently sucking your nipples, then gazing into your eyes. You know how it feels when a man gets distracted by your body, focusing on one part while forgetting that the rest of you exists. But this is very different. Your man's adoration of your body is obvious, but so is his depth of feeling. He feels and loves your form, but he feels and loves deeper than your form, too.

His kisses feel more like poetry reaching into your heart, a love offering of his deepest heart—preciously tendered by his knowledge of inevitable death—emerging through his lips to worship your breasts and so much deeper. You allow your body to respond to his worship. You press your open thighs around him, offering yourself to him more passionately, moaning and pleading, "Please, please…"

As he enters you sexually, your surrender unfolds beyond words, and you speak in tones of incoherent pleasure in response to his claim. He is still tender, but more forceful, filling you, hard, with his claiming thrust. Your vagina opens deeper, and his openness continues to fill your body. Your whole womb and belly open with fullness, and your heart opens, and your throat and mouth open, sounds of love emerging. Your love opens beyond your man's shape.

He stops moving. You open your eyes—you didn't even know you had closed them—and his gaze penetrates into you as deep as his thrusts. His gaze is demanding, wanting more from you, more depth, more love. You love to feel his demand. His belly still breathes full against your belly, pressing into you. Like a faultless dancer, his movements anticipate yours. You feel inhabited by his presence; he knows your heart deeper than you do.

For pleasure, you resist. You try to push, get out of his grasp, escape his weight. But he keeps you pinned beneath him. You push and push and he doesn't move, but enters you slowly, more deeply, filling your body and your heart while keeping you claimed to depth.

Then, you notice that his presence withdraws a bit. Is he thinking about something? Did you do something wrong? You free your wrist and dig your fingernails into his ass. That gets his attention. And now, as he looks into your eyes, he can feel your devotion, your yearning for more depth.

He realizes that his attention went shallow for a moment, but that your heart still waits deep. Your eyes softly plead for his deep entrance. You will not settle for less. If he goes shallow for even a fraction of a second, you awaken him present with your movements, a sound, or a slap. You offer your vulnerable heart to be taken by his claim. Your yearning is tangible. He can feel your heart's longing in the way you open your legs to him, in the sounds you make, in your eyes.

Your yearning draws him deeper, and when his claim commands your heart, you surrender more fully. Together, you go open without end. He feels into you, giving you everything, filling you so much you can't take any more, inhabiting your entire body, knowing your deepest heart's yearning. He feels through you, feeling open and still expressing his love as if this were your last moment on earth together. His presence is so deep and stable—his worship of your form goes through your form to the very openness of the moment—and you naturally surrender open in total trust.

Nothing is left but love, breathing, living, and opening as all.

5.

Spiritual
Sexiness

Your heart's light fills my life. Like all men, I may
occasionally look at a pretty woman and spend
hours toiling at work, but your heart is the source
of the radiance that inspires my entire life and
evokes my deepest gifts. Nothing opens my heart
more fully than seeing the light of love in your
eyes and feeling your body open as love to receive
me. Nothing is as beautiful as your heart's surrender and the radiant offering of your devotion.
Your love opens my heart endlessly, even when I
would otherwise forget love's depth.

Whether or not you are with a man, your heart yearns for deeper love. Often—but not always—you yearn for love through the form of a man. Why? And what makes you or a man sexy in a spiritual sense?

Your desire to be claimed by a man's deep love is based in the truth of your heart: You *are* love. Your love shines as light, so you want to be seen. Your love shows as the full force of surrender, so you want to be passionately entered. In truth, your deep heart is right *now* being claimed by openness, ravished by the openness of love.

Your yearning to be taken open is simply the natural feeling of your heart *already* being taken open, but you have patterns of resistance, and so you feel the tension—the longing—between the openness you deeply know is possible and the openness you are allowing.

Just as your love can open a man's heart, a deep man can offer you an opportunity to open more deeply.

Without even touching you, a deep man can swoon you open to God— he can open you to love's divine mystery and blissful benediction—if he is totally present with you, truly seeing you, feeling you, entering you with his loving desire, touching the most vulnerable depth of your heart.

When he looks into your eyes, you can feel him entering your heart. His presence can be so strong, so unwavering and passionate and clear, that his love invades you, deepening into you. Your body and heart open to him, surrendering open to receive his love, wanting him to enter you even deeper.

What you trust about a man is his integrity of being open in love with you and his strength of presence. When his attention wanders—he seems to be listening to you but his eyes are darting all over the room and his thoughts are elsewhere, or he is caught up in his own pursuit of pleasure—then you lose trust in him. In response to his lack of presence and integrity, your body tenses and your heart pulls back to protect itself.

But when his attention is totally with you—you can feel him feeling the rhythm of your breath, touching you just where you long to be caressed, anticipating your needs before you notice them—then you naturally surrender and open to receive him.

You crave his fully present attention, which results from the openness of his awareness, the freedom of his consciousness. Your man is spiritually sexy when his attention is free, when he is not wrapped up in a jangle of thoughts and conflicting desires, when his consciousness is free to be with you totally, undistracted.

Your man is spiritually sexy when you can feel his consciousness in his *entire body* fully alive and present with your entire body. His belly, legs, and feet are strongly present with you, not just his bulging eyes and genitals; his heart is fully feeling you through his whole body. His entire presence is unconvoluted, honest, and genuinely with you, and his whole body is open, relaxed, and strong with the force of conscious presence.

And what does he find spiritually sexy in you? He is irresistibly drawn into the light of your love, showing through your entire body as radiant openness and devotional surrender. When you fall in love with somebody, you become more radiant, and your friends can see it. Your eyes sparkle, your cheeks glow, your walk changes, becoming softer and more buoyantly alive. Light and life-energy is the way love appears through your body. Love's radiance, love's energy, shines and opens through your entire body in a very noticeable way.

The openness of this love-light is what your man finds spiritually sexy in you. The more you open in trust and offer this light through the yearning of your love, the more he wants to enter you and merge with your glorious surrender, his heart of presence melding as one with your heart of love. He wants to dive into your devotional surrender and take you open, more deeply, as your never-ending yearning invites him more deeply in to love's fullness.

Your capacity to open in oneness with a man's presence is your spiritual capacity for sexual surrender. Your man can feel whether or not you are surrendering open in yearning invitation for him to merge with your love-light and claim your heart. If you don't trust a man fully, then, of course, you won't surrender fully open with him.

Unsurrendered women attract unpresent men. Your lack of heart-surrender and your mistrust will make your man less present and less trustable. You and your man are either evoking in each other openness or closure, worship or distance. The depth of yearning you offer invites the depth of presence you are likely to get.

A man who could be fully present with you—a man whose consciousness was deep and clear because he was living his true purpose and his passionate heart was unencumbered by fear and ambiguity—such a man wants equally unambiguous surrender offered through your yearning body and heart. He wants your love offered as an open invitation with full energy through your entire body. You want his full presence entering your deep heart through his entire body.

Your man wants to see love shining in your face. He wants to feel your yearning rippling through your body, emerging through your moans of passion.

You want your man to truly see you, deeply feel you, and know you, utterly. You long for his claim to open you so deeply that your surrender is inevitable, love-forced beyond your own doing. Your heart and body open as the pleasure of almost unbearable devotional offering, "I am yours, take me."

You are only willing to surrender open if he is fully present with you, committed to claiming your heart with his absolute integrity of being. And he is only willing to commit his presence with you if you are willing to surrender open and offer your heart's light and devotion as love's yearning.

His presence will, in fact, waver, as will your offering of love's energy. You will sometimes feel unmet, and you will close down. And so you learn the art of breathing love and trusting open, as if surrendering open to sexual ravishment, with or without a man. All day, you can practice offering your heart and body to be claimed by God, settling for nothing less.

Your surrender and your man's commitment, opening each other more deeply than you would open yourselves, is an art that can be practiced in relationship. With or without a man, you can practice opening your body to flow with pleasure while opening your heart as an offering of love's yearning.

6.

Orgasmic Love

 ❧

Before I understood how to open with you, I tried giving you orgasms so I knew I was a good lover. But now, all I want is your surrender. I want your heart's pleasure to ripple through your open body and saturate my life with your love. Your body's openness to love's flow draws me into you, and through your heart's surrender I am opened to the love that lives as the universe. Whether you have an orgasm or not while we make love, your body's trust and devotional openness is my secret doorway to love's deepest bliss.

Your body's openness—your capacity to surrender open with your whole body so your heart can be ravished and taken by love—is a doorway to ecstatic spiritual depth, with or without a man. If your body can't open, your heart can't shine. When your body is surrendering open with pleasure from deep within, then you can open and offer your heart fully from the inside out.

Orgasm is one form of sexual pleasure. You may never have had what you call an orgasm, or you may have had many. It doesn't really matter. What matters is that your body can open in love's blissful surrender. If your pelvis is locked and your vagina is closed down or numb, then your heart is prevented from offering love fully through your body.

Opening through orgasmic surrender, alone or with a lover, can provide a unique opportunity to offer your deepest love and uninhibited yearning through your fully expressed body.

CLITORAL ORGASMS

You may or may not have a man in your life, but for now, imagine that you are in bed with your lover. He strokes your belly and caresses your breasts. He touches you gently inside your thighs, trailing his fingertips from knee to crotch. Fondling, touching, loving, he eventually kisses you between your legs. With sensitivity and skill, he licks, nibbles, and sucks your most sensitive flesh, while also touching your feet and legs and belly and breasts with his hands.

Your breath becomes shorter and faster. Your eyes close. You grab his hair and push his face tightly against you. Breathing rapidly, an orgasm seizes through your body, your voice high-pitched, shrieking, your face tense, your body tightening, and then relaxing, after one or two or three clitoral orgasms.

These are the most superficial orgasms, requiring little if any emotional or spiritual trust—a vibrator can be used to achieve this pleasure. Nevertheless, clitoral orgasms can prepare you for surrendering open more deeply.

VAGINAL OR G-SPOT ORGASMS

You have been making love for almost an hour, your lover thrusting in and out, his body pressing against yours, while kissing you, biting your neck, and pinning you beneath him with his loving strength. "Don't stop," you groan, as your body relaxes open. Your arms spread out from your sides, your heart opens, your mouth opens. Your moans are long and deep from your belly.

As the waves begin, your sound goes deeper. You gaze into your lover's eyes, moist with vulnerable affection, your bodies softening into each other, your hearts melding. You take him in more deeply, opening your body to him, giving yourself to him, yielding fully. You gush between your legs, your vagina grabbing him, milking him, pulling him in more deeply.

His constant rhythmic loving sends a purr through your body like a cat vibrating. You relax more deeply open, and waves of open pleasure begin radiating from your vagina out through your whole body. Like an ocean of openness, your pleasure draws him in deeper. You offer your heart to him, unprotected. Your soft bodies press together, your hips moving in uncontrollable waves, your mouth ohh-ing in open pleasure, your body surrendering layer after layer more open than you have in a long time.

The G-Spot, an area of spongy tissue a few inches inside the anterior or front part of the vagina, is very sensitive in many women. If you are capable of experiencing G-Spot orgasms, but haven't yet, this tissue can hold much tension, anger, and pain. This area of your vagina can be massaged according to your verbal guidance—slower, harder, softer, faster—eventually relaxing you enough to open in deep orgasmic waves, possibly even ejaculating fluids from this spongy tissue.

CERVICAL ORGASMS

Your cervix is the physical source of extraordinarily deep orgasms. As with your G-Spot, your cervix may be quite sensitive and painful to the touch if you haven't regularly allowed full pleasure to move through your cervical area.

But with a few weeks of receiving massage near your cervix, this area opens. And if you have a man in your life, then when you make love, as your lover's thrust stimulates and opens your cervical area, your emotional and spiritual surrender can lead to tremendous orgasmic revelations of love's bliss.

After an hour of heart-connected, passionate, sexual merger, imagine that your loving together with your man continues. His entrance into your body is deep, persistent, creative, unyielding. His strong hands hold your wrists, his belly presses deeply down into yours, his gentle force enters you again and again, opening you, opening places you have never felt to open.

You feel utterly claimed, taken open to God, obliterated in his deep loving. You let go even more deeply, dying in the intensity of his loving, crying as all love bursts you open. You are killed by bliss, softly, sweetly pervaded by his tender love. Your skin dissolves. Your edges melt. And again, even deeper, you let go of something you didn't know you were holding, a minute clench deep in your heart opens, giving open to him, to God, and your tears flow.

Forgetting beginning and end, your orgasm opens deeper and deeper. Layers of surrender are offered up through your depths, out through your body, as he penetrates you to gone. Together, you open as such deep love all disappears in the fullness of bliss, light melting all hold, love filling all space, an unbearable fullness surrendering open endlessly, boundlessly, abundantly, no place remaining unopened, untouched, unrevealed.

Your orgasm unfolds and unfolds as never before, love rippling you open, your face drenched in tears, your body in sweat, bright beyond form. You are being breathed open in blissful death, ravished open, unable to hold on, surrendered open by a force you *are* so deeply, the living light of love that you always almost knew now shines so fully, wracking you open in unbearable pleasure, your deepest womb grasping and letting go, seizing and releasing, the pulse of the universe opening out from deep between your legs, opening out from deep within your belly, your heart given open fully, all of you given, offered in utter devotional surrender.

For days, love's bliss flows freely through your body. Your motions are full of grace, your face shining, smooth, and radiant with love's flow. Your lover and your friends can feel this orgasm's openness continuing to resound through your gestures, the way you walk, the expression in your eyes, the relaxed tone of your voice, surrendering you open for a long time after the sexual occasion has ended.

Surrendering open to the fullest flow of pleasure can be an important part of opening fully and offering your deepest love to the world and to your man if you are in a relationship. With practice and skill, solo or with a partner, your orgasmic capacity deepens along with other aspects of your capacity to offer your deepest heart. Over time, you may experience deep orgasms without any sexual stimulation at all, simply while dancing, or doing yoga, or breathing fully and offering yourself open to God to take.

Your body is built to be opened by love and to open as love's offering. Love is who you are, and love is the gift you are born to give. With practice, you can learn to live open as devotional fullness, as if you were receiving deep sexual ravishment and offering your heart's fullest gifts through your whole body.

How would you be breathing right now, sitting right now, moving right now, if your body were being entered by a man of enormous love and integrity, a man who felt so deeply into your heart that you were forced to reveal your most subtle closure, taking you open so exquisitely you could hardly bear to open in so much love and trust?

To live open, your body can practice feeling sexually open, whether or not you are having a physical orgasm or even having sex. Through sex and in everyday life, you can practice feeling, breathing, and offering yourself open as if the passionate force of a divine lover were entering you sexually, opening your heart and body as wide as the universe shines.

7.

Love and Fear

❧

You and I both have our excuses for not opening in love with each other. Still, both of our hearts yearn to open and commune in love. I want to make this commitment with you: I will do my best to open through my fears and truly see you, feel you, and bloom you open to God with my love. Will you meet me in this commitment? Will you promise to open and give your love's offering as best as you can, even when you are afraid or hurt? If we can each commit to opening, there is no limit to how deeply our love can grow or how fully our gifts may flower.

Your secret sexual desire is to be ravished, lovingly forced open in unbearable pleasure, and taken fully open to God by a man of deep spiritual wisdom, strength, humor, sensitivity, and integrity. But your past relationships probably fell short of your deepest desire for a man's loving, and your current relationship is probably also lacking. Why?

The love that is deep in your heart is probably buried under layers of frustration and pain. How did these layers harden around the open yearning of your heart?

Since you were a young woman, you have probably dreamed of being lovingly *taken* by a good man, a man who could truly know you and cherish your heart, a man of deep integrity, a man you could trust with your life—a man you could trust to take you open into love's deepest bliss. Even now, you probably yearn to be taken by a man who truly sees your deepest heart's bright love and really knows your body, staying in touch with your unique energy as it moves and changes.

Sometimes—perhaps rarely—your lover can be so present with you that your fears relax and your body opens. In these magic moments, you and your lover connect so deeply that your hearts merge as one. All separation dissolves. Your body is given over to him, and his tender strength opens you further than you can control. You may weep and tremble in his arms, beneath his body, held in his love, pressed open by the force of his true desire for your deepest heart.

These moments are special, and few. Eventually, your man probably betrays you, either because he desires another woman more than you or because his love becomes shallow, his sexual neediness disgusting. Even in moments of intimacy, he doesn't touch your deepest heart or even try. You know he can love you open, perhaps more than any man ever has, and yet, over time, he becomes less interested in communing with your deepest heart. He drifts into his career, focusing on his projects, sitting in front of the TV, or satisfying his need for superficial sexual release.

So you begin to learn to live with your hurt and take care of yourself. If you can't depend on a man's love, then you can only depend on yourself. You learn to take control of your life, to guide yourself to your own destination. But something is still missing, no matter how successful your career or how comfortable your life is. You still yearn to be taken by a man's real love, to be truly seen and opened by your lover's penetrating gaze, touch, and profound heart-desire.

Secretly, you still yearn to surrender to a man who is worthy of your trust. But you have not met him—and worse, you have learned that when you surrender open and give yourself completely to a man, you eventually get hurt. In the rare moments when your depth is invited, your pain comes up first and you often end up scaring your man away.

So, you begin to doubt love. You lose trust in men. You surround your wounded heart with shells of emotional protection, hopefully preventing more hurt. Your body develops tensions and even diseases after years of not surrendering, not receiving deep love, not giving yourself entirely, as you so long to do with every cell of your being. There is always tension—the tension of not being met and really stretched open in the fullness of the love you are.

So when a man feels you, he feels your shells. In your face, he sees the strain of long hours or years of holding your life together while your deepest heart would rather have surrendered open in ecstatic trust. In your gait, he feels the stress of unoffered bodily devotion, while your deep heart would rather have been a slave to love, commanded open by love's torrential flow, undulated by love's boundless pleasure. Around your heart, he senses the "do not trespass" warning, and so he holds himself back from entering your life deeply.

Few men are capable of entering a woman's heart and opening her body to God's bliss, but few women are capable of offering their heart and body to be claimed open in this way. Fear is the feeling of refusal. Fear is the feeling of mistrust. Fear is the heart's contraction that withdraws openness behind walls of protection. Fear is the act of unlove, the negation of love, the refusal to open and offer love's openness as your gift. Anything less than a life of total loving is fear.

Fear—the refusal to open as love—is the only reason your sexual life and relationship are less than God-blissful. Fear forms shells around your heart and closes your body so that love cannot move deeply into you, claiming you, opening you, allowing you to trust deeper than your sense of self. If you trusted and received love more deeply, you would naturally surrender open, alive as the most powerful force in the world: the devotional offering of love.

Men are terrified of a woman's depth of love and the energy that moves as a woman's sexuality and emotions. And, at the same time, men want nothing more in this life than to merge completely with a woman's devotional love and wild energy. Only as a man outgrows his fear can he handle a woman's tremendous love-energy without running. And only such a man is worthy of your devotional offering in a committed intimacy.

Most men can't meet you fully. So, though your heart and body yearn to be ravished by real love, you bury your heart's longing under a life of busyness, family, friends, and distractions. You learn to plod on and get things done. You learn to seal off from your own longing. You occupy yourself with chores and to-do lists. You focus on your financial goals, or perhaps you decide to give your life to serving a social cause or following a spiritual path. You spend time with your friends, enjoy travel, exercise and take care of yourself. And still, your heart yearns, whether you are alone or with a man who is not deeply claiming your heart.

Just as you have chosen to guard your heart for fear of being hurt, the man you attract will have chosen to claim life more shallowly than his true depth. He drifts uncommitted to total love because he is afraid of losing what seems like his freedom.

Your relationship won't work because his freedom is false and your love is hidden; you are both afraid. You are unwilling to offer yourself completely without protection, so you attract a man without the capacity or willingness to claim you completely.

A commitment to love requires opening beyond these fears. Your lover's willingness to inhabit your life as his own, to feel your heart deeply and claim you open to love's deepest bliss, must grow—just as your willingness must grow to offer your life and heart as love, even though you know you will be hurt and betrayed in the future.

Even if you don't have a lover in your life or if your lover doesn't seem able to meet your heart with his full loving presence, you can learn to keep your heart open to the flow of love. Your heart may hurt, your heart may yearn for a deeper way to give and receive love with your man, but your heart-practice is to relax open, breathing and feeling in connection with your lover and all beings. At heart, everybody wants only to give and receive love.

You can practice keeping your heart open for the sake of love's fullness, even when your man hurts you, even when you are alone, even when the pain and yearning in your heart feel overwhelming. For the sake of love's fullest flow, you can allow your heart to yearn open, deeply receiving and offering love without closing down to protect itself.

Then, your life is moved not so much by your man's needs nor by your own needs of self-reliance, but by the deep wisdom-flow of love, which is alive as you and at the heart of all beings. You are fulfilled neither by a man's attention nor by taking care of yourself, but by opening as love, feeling the heart of everyone, offering your heart open so love can move you as it will, offering your life as a gift of love to all, including your chosen man.

All the moments of your life—making a business deal, caring for your children, arguing with your lover—can be a dance of love's emergence, an opportunity for opening your heart and offering your life to flow open as love's wisdom, love's power, and love's indestructible vulnerability.

To live with an open heart and body moved by love is your only option if you want to fulfill your deepest desire—to receive and give love's most full bliss—with or without a man.

8.

Your Sexual Essence

I have chosen you as my lover for many reasons. But I am most compelled by the attraction I feel for your feminine heart. I appreciate many of your qualities such as your intelligence, your sense of humor, and your insight—but I also appreciate those things in my close friends, my brothers and sisters, even my colleagues at work.

Your special gift to me is the unique quality of the feminine love you offer. Your feminine essence fills my life with a love that is so intimate and tender, my heart opens at your sight. I understand there is a lot more to you, but you are my chosen lover—rather than just my friend—because the ambrosial light of your feminine essence fills my heart and brightens

my world with beauty, inspiration, and the
unending grace of love's abundance.

You embody both masculine and feminine qualities, although you may express them in different proportions at different times in your life.

If you find it easy to navigate toward your goals but more difficult to dance in whole-body ecstasy, then your masculine qualities are probably more highly developed than your feminine.

If you find it easy to flow while moving with sensual pleasure—while shopping, dancing, making love, and talking with friends—but more difficult to carry out long-term projects, then your feminine is probably more highly developed than your masculine.

Each person can develop both masculine and feminine qualities within him or her. With your masculine, you can learn to direct your life with great clarity and discipline toward very specific goals as a way to offer your deepest heart's gift to the world. With your feminine, you can learn to flow lovingly in the midst of chaos—a room full of playing children, a friend sobbing in emotional panic—offering your oceanic energy and fullness as a deep love-gift from your heart.

Although you have both masculine and feminine qualities and gifts, at your core you have a unique sexual essence. Your sexual essence is your sexual identity. It has nothing to do with the gender of your body. Man or woman, your sexual essence is determined by what your heart identifies with most deeply: the unfolding drama of the *ever-changing flow of love and dance of life's light* or the mission toward *unchanging and eternal freedom of consciousness*.

Do you identify more with love's ebb and flow in your heart or the adventure toward freedom? At the movies, do you cry more at love stories or at films about justice and conquering all odds against an enemy to be free? Are you more moved by love's drama or freedom's mission?

Which words of your lover turn you on more, sexually? Imagine that your lover says to you, "I trust you and your mission, and I will follow you anywhere." Now imagine that he says, "I love you and cherish the beauty of light that I see in you, and I claim your deepest heart as mine, forever."

If you have a *masculine sexual essence*, then you are turned on by a lover who trusts your direction so much he is willing to surrender to your claim, submit ecstatically to your strength of penetrative love, and follow you anywhere.

If you have a *feminine sexual essence*, then you are turned on by a lover who sees the beauty of your heart's light and who feels your love's depth, worshipping your radiant heart with his integrity, passionately claiming your life with his strong presence.

A person who has a masculine essence revels in challenge, facing death, and overcoming all odds to succeed in a mission of freedom, whether that is a quest for financial, political, artistic, or spiritual liberation. Even watching sports—which are ritualized wars, challenges, or fights for freedom—can be so emotionally moving that a masculine-essence person often shouts and screams more during a football game than while making love. Is this more like you, or more like your lovers, past and present?

Most (but not all) women have a sexual essence that is more feminine than masculine, although the exact proportions vary and each person's sexual essence is unique. Though you may enjoy using your masculine gifts to succeed in the world, deep down you probably have a more feminine essence that yearns for the flow of love more than a fight for freedom, although you may still feel uncertain about what you really want.

Your masculine "go" and feminine "flow" can be gifts, but they can also be used to create shells of safety and protection, confusing you and preventing your true sexual essence from offering your deepest love and gifts to your man, your family, your friends, and the world. You can inadvertently hide behind your schedule book and the challenges of your career, while your true sexual essence yearns to be seen and touched, your body aches to be taken, and the deepest heart of your love remains unnoticed and ungiven.

You can seem stressfully concerned about *where* you are going in your life, even though, deep down, you may be much more concerned about *who* you are going with and *how* love is flowing. You can get caught up in the masculine fight toward liberation and your mission toward freedom, even though the deep bliss of love, or its lack, is much more central to your feminine heart's fullness.

Your concern for career and self-sufficiency is obviously healthy, but your deepest fulfillment may await risking your heart wide open, offering your bright love to all beings, and giving yourself to be claimed—by a man of integrity, by a family of beloveds, by a world that needs your love. Love is the only way to live that won't leave your feminine heart feeling unseen, ungiven, empty, and wanting—no matter how successful your professional life may be.

9.

Your True Heart and Its Shells

Like every man or woman, sometimes I want to flow and enjoy feminine energy and sometimes I want to go straight ahead toward a goal in the masculine style with no interruptions. But my sexual essence happens to be masculine, and so I am attracted to you, a lover with a feminine essence.

I know what I want sexually from you, dear lover. I want to see your feminine light and feel your invitation to merge with your feminine energy. I want to enter and claim your feminine heart open to God. I want to inhabit your loving surrender and open in love's bliss with you not simply as friends, but as lovers in the play of passion and ravishment.

And yet I often feel you closing down or pushing me away. Sexually, I sometimes feel your coldness and resistance more than your joy of surrender. I know that sometimes it is my fault. I have been insensitive or cruel. And I know sometimes you are just too tired to open. But there are times that I don't feel your heart open to receive my love even when you seem full of energy and I am fully present with you.

I want to enjoy deep sexual loving with you, but I also want both of us to open for the sake of everyone. I want our <u>bedroom to be a palace of bliss, but I also want our hearts to give their gifts all day</u>, so we live as the fulfillment of love, always opening, feeling everyone, making love through all our daily actions and relationships. I want you to open to me and I want to give you everything, but I also want both of us to open, feel, and offer ourselves to everyone all day.

I hope that together we can liberate our true hearts from our cages of fear. Then, our bodies can merge open in sexual delight and our hours can come and go as love all day.

If you are like most women, you were born with a more feminine sexual essence. At heart, you are more identified with ever-changing life than with changeless death—as a child you enjoyed playing house more than playing war. You enjoyed playing with puppies and colors and make-up and flavors. You enjoyed getting clothing and jewelry—rather than weapons and games of challenge—for birthday presents. You loved to be seen, because you are identified with love's light. Anything that adorns your light—sequins, sparkles, bangles—magnifies your happiness.

As a young woman, you may have dreamt of masculine saviors: horses, pop stars, white knights—any animal or human, real or imaginary, that could take you somewhere new, somewhere magic. Deep in your heart, you felt that someday a man would see your true beauty, your true light, your boundless ocean of love, and take you to the place you always wanted to be: surrendered open like the sky filled with moonlight, taken by your beloved into the bright domain of love's bliss.

But at some point, you probably stopped trusting the yearning of your own feminine heart. You may have absorbed the anti-feminine attitude of your culture. Or possibly your family strongly emphasized masculine values.

For one reason or another, you probably became convinced that it is better—stronger—to navigate for yourself, to take yourself somewhere rather than trust to be taken by love. You became suppressed in your desire to be seen and worshipped as love's light. You came to believe that guiding your life's direction is more important than trusting the fathomless love-wisdom that flows naturally from your deepest heart's radiance.

Maybe your parents found your little sister more pretty than you, so you protected your crushed heart with a shell of masculine ambition: "My little sister may be pretty, but I'm going to be a scientist!" Perhaps you felt how your mother was restricted and belittled by your father, so you protected your vulnerable heart with a shell of masculine control: "Nobody is going to tell *me* what to do. I'm going to be the captain of my own ship!"

If you chose to be a scientist because you loved science, or you chose to navigate your own life because that was your greatest bliss, then such decisions would be healthy and heart fulfilling. But if you chose to be a scientist because your parents ignored your radiance and your heart was crushed, or if you chose to guide your own life because you didn't want to be hurt like your mother was, then you have created shells built of fear rather than a life moved by the openness of love.

As you grow from childhood to your teenage years, you may build yet another shell. You want boys to be interested in you. However, the attractive brightness of your feminine radiance remains hidden behind your shells of fear-based masculine directionality that surround your crushed and unacknowledged heart. So, on top of this acquired masculine shell of protection, you begin to create a shell of superficial feminine expression.

You buy the jeans that all the popular girls at school are wearing, checking out your butt in the mirror, wondering if this will get the boys to want you. You spend hours purchasing and trying on not only clothing but also jewelry, fragrances, and make-up—not as loving adornments of your abundant radiance, but because you feel love lacking. You feel unseen and unworthy because the masculine shell you acquired as a child is hiding the full love and true shine of your heart.

Your true feminine heart of vulnerable love-radiance—crushed or negated in childhood—has become surrounded by a masculine shell of fear: "Because my love-light is inadequate, I'll direct my life toward success so I am worthy of love." In your teenage years, a feminine shell of fear is then added: "Unless I make my surface shine, boys won't notice me."

Already, as a teenager, the love-radiance of your true feminine essence is hidden behind a masculine shell of protective and assertive directionality and a feminine shell of superficial "see me," lack of self-worth, and covert manipulation of men's attention.

Beneath all your shells, your deep heart is always full of love's light. So, at heart, showing open as light and flowing open as love's offering is the most ecstatic and true way to live. But your acquired shells have their own voice: "Beauty is only skin deep." "My mind is more important than my body." "I can't trust men." "If I want a man's love I've got to make him want me." "My professional goals are more crucial to my life's happiness than who I go with or how much love I offer through my life and every breath."

These are all lies, and your deep feminine heart knows it. Yet, you are confused, because your shells can be so strong. You can come to believe the lies of your shells, and therefore, you can live an entire life betraying your deepest desire: to be recognized as light, adored and worshipped as love's radiance, offering yourself as a gift of love to be claimed by true divine masculine integrity, ravished open to God by love's deepest claim of your heart.

Perhaps you try to trust a man and he eventually leaves you. Again you feel betrayed, so now, again from fear, you build yet another shell—"independent career woman"—that will protect you from being hurt or left in the cold by a man's untrustable commitment. If your career is an expression of your love, then your heart can be fully offered through your profession. But if you are building a career because you are afraid of being hurt and abandoned again, then fear is woven into the foundation of your choices, and your career will always be tainted by doubt, loneliness, stress, and lack of heart-fulfillment.

Your radiant feminine heart of love may now be surrounded by a shell of masculine impetus (because your sister was prettier than you or masculine values were more important in your family), which is surrounded by a shell of feminine gloss (because your surface is what boys look at), which is surrounded by a shell of masculine ambition (because you are afraid of being financially dependent on a man again).

These shells may have become rigidified in your body, so your orgasms are shallow and your face creased with tension. These shells confuse your mind with conflicting desires, now for independence and safety, now to be swept off your feet by a dangerous man, now to succeed on your own. These shells block your genuine emotional currents, so you feel stuck, sometimes numb, sometimes enraged, sometimes hysterical, but not very often does your deepest ocean of love-light spontaneously emerge as free, unobstructed waves of heart-open emotional flow, with the universe or with a man.

Furthermore, your shells attract men with reciprocal shells, men who have long ago lost touch with their deep masculine heart of truth, purpose, and impeccable loving. Shells of lies surround your crushed heart, so you attract men who are also crushed at heart and who are surrounded by lies. These men lie not only to you, but also to themselves. These men *live* a lie, just like you do.

Probably, deep in your heart, you dream of being with a man of great integrity, a lover of such care, strength, humor, wisdom, and depth of love that you can trust him utterly, surrendering wide open to be blissfully taken further open by love's ravishing force, so your deepest heart is exposed to God's infinite joy, and your body blooms in uncontrollable waves of divine pleasure.

And yet, you may *feel* more balanced—equally moved by masculine and feminine motivations—because step by step throughout your life you have betrayed your heart's deepest desire as you acquired shells of fear that create confusion, neutralizing your deepest heart's yearning.

One shell is built of your fear of being dependent, so it drives you to achieve a sense of emotional autonomy and self-reliance. Another shell is built of your fear that you are not attractive enough, so it causes you to compare yourself to other women, dressing and acting in ways to attract men even though you wouldn't trust most men to enter you anyway, so you protect your heart and body even as you do your best to hook men's attention.

You want the freedom to dress however you want; you want men to respect you as a person and not treat you like an object; you want men to find you sexy but not harass you; you want a trustable man to commit his love to you; you want a man to give you space and honor your own decisions; you know you are capable of deep love; you hold back your love because your heart is afraid of being hurt again; you move your body with masculine direction to achieve financial independence; you are tired and stressed and your feminine body is aching to be loved beneath your mistrust—all of your shells blur together and neutralize the true sexual gifts of your essence.

yes

So when a man feels you, he no longer feels your deep gifts of love, but your shells. He feels your desire for independence and your desire to be wanted. He feels your push and your pull. He feels moments when your heart surrenders to be taken, and moments when your protection shields your heart from being hurt.

He is probably as confused about his deepest purpose as you are about your deepest desire for love. So, instead of persisting in committed loving, peeling away layer after layer of your resistance, lovingly claiming your true sexual essence so you can offer your open heart as a divine gift—instead, he casually enjoys what he can and moves on to a less complicated woman; you appear to be quite attached to your independence, anyway.

yikes!

You may indeed have a genuinely balanced sexual essence—a small percentage of women do—but chances are you actually have a feminine sexual essence that is neutralized by layer after layer of acquired masculine and feminine shells of fear, and so you are creating confusion: What is your deepest heart's desire?

If you have a feminine sexual essence, then you want to be truly seen, entered at heart, opened as love, and danced by love's light. You are the aspect of this moment's divine revelation that shows Herself as love's radiance, and, naturally, you yearn to be taken by your man's trustable, penetrating presence deeper and wider than you can bear, blissfully. Likewise, he yearns to merge with your light. This yearning reveals itself as the one divine openness of love knowing itself through two bodies.

You want to be ravished by your lover's desire to enter you and merge with your heart, and he wants to be invited by your surrender, the display of your body's pleasure and the offering of your heart to be taken, entered, and opened beyond form. This is how two human bodies become one openness of love, expressing the divine revelation of consciousness and light, the interpenetrating He and She of every moment. This is true sex and divinity.

True sex is about divine intimate communion, heart-to-heart worship, opening as love's bliss, offering your deepest gifts to each other. This two-bodied sexual offering prepares you for opening beyond yourself so you can offer your deepest gifts in every moment to *all* beings, opening as love's light through *every* body.

With practice, your man learns to take every moment open to love's depth, fearlessly and relentlessly, and you learn to fully receive every moment deeply into your heart—so you are actively receiving the ravishment of divine presence, pleasurably "forced" open by the moment's thick fullness, offering your heart's radiant surrender to enlighten the world alive as uninhibited love.

As you grow more open as love's fullest offering, you still enjoy your career, your success, and your life's direction as much as you want, but you don't forget your heart's *deepest* desire—you no longer negate your heart's yearning to give and receive love, to be claimed open to God's depth and offered open as love's light through the heart of all beings.

Eventually, you realize that self-sufficiency is a transition phase. You are not responsible only for yourself; you are responsible for everyone. Your heart naturally opens with and feels other hearts. Your heart naturally responds to the heart-yearning of others. Instead of denying your own needs or limiting your love to self-reliant independence, you realize that, more than anything else, you actually yearn to live open as a devotional offering of love.

Are you ready to feel your heart's deepest yearning and the yearning at everyone's heart: to receive love, to give love, to live open as love's fullest light?

You may choose to be a corporate executive, an attorney, or a baker. You may choose to raise a family, start a school, or manage an organization. What you do with your life is less important than how you live it: encased in shells of fear or wide open, actively receiving God's immense weight of love, ravished to your heart's core by deeply feeling every moment's divine intensity and presence, offering your love to enlighten the hearts of all those around you, including your lover.

10.

Offering or Betraying Your Heart

As much as I love you, we are not alone. Through loving you, I have learned to open my heart and feel everyone's heart. Their love is my love, as is yours. Their suffering is my suffering, as is yours. Just as I am committed to loving you open to God, I am compelled to claim the world as my lover who I must do my best to enter and open to God.

I am afraid, at times, to enter you and the world. I shrivel and seek refuge in private comforts. I can feel your response to my offering or my lack. When I shrink and hold back my gifts, your face shows pain. When I feel through my fear and offer everything I can for the sake of opening you and the world to God, then your face shines with love's brightness.

I see everything in you. I see my fear and
courage reflected in your face, but I also feel
everyone's resistance and invitation reflected
in your body. You are so sensitive, dear lover.
Your body is so ready to open into the shape
of your surroundings. But with me and others
you have often been encircled by love's lack. I
can feel years of love's absence still hardened in
your body, and I so want to feel you open and
receive my love.

The fairy tale has asked you to believe that if you find the right man and give him what he wants and needs, then he will love you forever. But it doesn't work out that way. You can't depend on his love. He either wanders to women he finds more attractive than you, or he stays with you, but doesn't continue to enter your heart deeply. He may even want to love you deeply, but he doesn't know how.

Your lover probably isn't aware of the constant suffering you experience due to his shallow presence. He is sitting next to you—or lying on top of you—and still he is trapped in his own thoughts, his own sensations, his grid-like world of projects, goals, and plans. His emotions seem so narrow—he's happy when he's succeeding in life and unhappy when he's failing—and your emotions seem so full, wide, and extreme. He runs away when you allow your emotions to flow unconstrained. He can't really deal with your full emotional strength and sexual desire for depth. He might even think you are crazy.

In the end, whether the two of you separate for what you both hope are greener pastures or whether you stay together—seemingly satisfied on the outside but dying, yearning for more, on the inside—you eventually settle for less than your heart knows is possible. You adapt the minutes of your day to working, taking care of your family, and talking with friends. And at the end of the day, in bed with your lover or alone, you are exhausted and stressed from living a lie, your body not undulating in pleasure, your heart not blown-open as all-light. Your deepest love is waiting, waiting, fading.

MEN BECOME AMBIGUOUS AND LESS PRESENT

If your man's heart is surrounded by shells, then he loses touch with his life's truth, his deep heart-direction. He begins to live a lie. He knows he isn't giving his deepest gift to you or the world. He knows he has sold out on his real dream. He has settled for comfort and security.

Nothing hurts a man's heart more than feeling that he does not know his deepest purpose—or if he does, that he's afraid to live it. So, if your man is like most, his deep heart is suffering tremendously—not because of a lack of intimacy in his relationship, but because he feels lost and he knows he is wasting his life.

He is afraid to potentially lose the comfort and security of his family, home, money, or health, so he holds back from doing the only thing that will cure his heart's pain: He is afraid to commit his life to discovering his deepest truth, uncovering his deepest gift, and giving his deepest love without compromise to you, his family, and the entire world. He is afraid to be free of fear since it will cost him everything he has ever acquired or known.

The only way for a man to be free is to die in every moment, to let go of everything, feel the deepest truth of his heart, and offer himself to you and everyone without holding back. His depth of consciousness, expressed through his unique gifts, is all he has to offer, and it is all you really want. You want his undivided presence, his true and genuine love-commitment, his heart exposed and wide open to feel yours.

When your man is offering you or the world less than his deepest truth, you can feel it, and you suffer the stress of his ambiguity and fear. When you are intimate with a man who is living this kind of lie—acting out a pretend life of comfort and security yet ungiven from his true heart—how could you open to him sexually?

How could you open your heart and body fully to a man who doesn't even know what his heart truly wants? Naturally, your heart and body close to such a man, protecting your deepest openness from being violated by a man's ambiguous poke. Even though you may truly love your man, you are also disgusted by his false face, his lack of depth, genuine commitment, and heart-direction.

To survive, your man has probably numbed himself to the horrible pain of not knowing his deepest purpose. He has spent years in trivial pursuits of shallow goals, and has settled for whatever success he has managed to acquire. Yet, you can feel he is lost, no matter how successful he tells himself he is.

You are exquisitely sensitive to his deep potential—his genuine gifts and fully offered heart—and you are equally sensitive to his self-deception, the way he lies to himself, the distance he creates between himself and his own heart's desire, and between himself and your heart's desire. This distance hurts you. His false satisfaction hurts you. His numbness to his own suffering and to yours frustrates you, eventually evoking your anger. You want his fullness—not only for you but also for his own sake and the sake of all beings—and he seems unable to even feel what you are talking about.

When your man lives behind shells of fear rather than opening and offering his heart's deepest offering, his consciousness becomes weakened and shielded in numbness fed by lies sustained by shallow ambition.

With time, your man's presence retracts into his own little world. You can't feel him with you, even when he is entering you sexually. Of course your sexual life is shallow—your man has become shallow, and he can't even feel it anymore, so thoroughly have his shells encased his heart.

WOMEN BECOME BODILY STRESSED AND HEART-CLOSED

To protect your own heart from being inadvertently raped by your self-centered lover's lack of feeling and awareness, you have put up your own walls. Your deep vagina is resistant to his mechanical thrusts. Your heart is shielded from his disconnected words of criticism and insult. Every time you try to open to your man, he diminishes your experience, as if your feelings were wrong, sick, or *your* problem.

He asks you how you are feeling, but your feelings are too huge and complex to squeeze into a simple answer. So he abuses you with more questions, convincing you that you are too dependent on him, that you need to be more responsible for yourself, and that your "emotional problems" are your own and have nothing to do with him.

Your experience is that his heart is yours; how he lives his life—even the nuances of where his attention goes, if he fidgets, or his subtle changes in tone of voice—affects your heart intensely. He seems to be able to live in a self-enclosed world where he can pursue his goals apart from whatever is happening with you. However, your heart is directly linked to his, as if threads of feeling were connecting the two of you, so your heart soars or sinks with his heart—and so does your trust.

This is not a weakness on your part, although your man may try to convince you that it is. Your feminine heart is much more sensitive to the flow of energy and emotion than his masculine heart. In fact, your heart is much more responsive to the depth of his consciousness—how present or not he is with you and in his life—than he is. He is numb to his own lack of presence and blind to how he actively shallows his heart, wrapping up his attention in trivial but all-consuming projects and thoughts.

Your heart-sensitivity can be a great gift to him. Your suffering, fully and responsively expressed, can teach him much about how his self-enclosed and unfeeling consciousness is paining the entire world. Your heart's vulnerable strength can inspire his deepest gifts and evoke his commitment to open and give his love to you and the world without fear—which is the freedom he most deeply desires. But you can only help him if *you* are open.

Chances are, after years of shallow men, you have closed to protect yourself from constant heart suffering. Otherwise, you would have gone insane. Every time your man drifts, scratches an itch unconsciously, wastes time in front of the TV, pretends to be intimate with you but actually is preoccupied in his own thoughts and sensations—every time your man is less than fully present with you or betraying his own depth, holding back his gifts in fear and numbness, your heart is crushed.

So, you have probably trained yourself to feel less. You can lay beneath a man while he humps you and at least derive a bit of shallow clitoral pleasure—amidst the tragic heart-pain of not being ravished open to God by his feeling-force and deep presence. You can sit and listen to your man talk about his stupid projects without shouting and screaming, "Wake up! Open your heart! You are wasting your life and killing me with your mediocrity!"

Your hurt and anger are hidden beneath shells of civilized stress: You pursue your own interests, spend time with your friends, and try not to complain too much to your man. If you let out what you really feel about how he treats you, you would either scare him away with your churning anguish or chop his head off with your rage.

But at least he is willing to share a home with you, at least you share a decent life, so it's not worth risking what you *do* share for the sake of what you most deeply desire. You are betraying your deepest heart as much as your man is. You are settling for shallow love just like your man is settling for shallow purpose. You both know there is a deeper way to live, yet you are both holding back your deepest gifts of love, not offering yourselves fully to each other or to the world.

His shallowness expresses itself as ambiguity, purposelessness, and lack of presence. Yours shows itself through your body. Your shells of protection literally enclose your heart, your vagina, your belly—all the most vulnerable and soft parts of your flesh are hardened against the barrage of insult, abuse, and rejection that your man's aimless thrusts cause you.

The most feminine parts of your body may become diseased, or at least closed down to pleasure. Your energy becomes blocked, your emotions suppressed. Your true heart's desire gets buried so deeply that you may no longer even hope for anything more than a decent relationship. Your deep desire to be taken, ravished, opened, and blissfully offered to God as unbounded love has all but disappeared behind years of devastation, frustration, and betrayal.

You and your man are no longer hoping to be fulfilled by someone else. You have grown beyond dependence. But you are probably stuck in a phase of self-reliance. You have probably become trapped in the belief that you can only make yourself happy: You are responsible for your own happiness, your lover is responsible for his, and to give your heart without holding back any in reserve for yourself is a sign of weakness. This results in a terrible and constant sense of separation.

Beyond the needs for dependence and independence, you can learn to love so your shells soften and you grow open without protection. Your deepest heart's desire can be allowed to percolate up from your depths and express your genuine love outward through every part of your body. As you learn to tenderly open your shells of protection, you can actively receive the ravishment you have always wanted and fully offer your love as a gift to all.

When you are ready, you can open beyond the safety of self-responsibility for one body. You can merge open in two-bodied sexual devotion. You can open to feel and breathe all—your lover, your family, your friends, every-one—in the full offering of your heart's openness.

You can live as divine love, opening and breathing as this entire moment. You can offer your life as if this moment's presence were entering you deeply like a lover's intense claim, your body danced by love's unblocked currents, your heart open as an offering, breathing as far as you can see and feel. You can open as the love that lives as all.

11.

The Two-Bodied
Play of Love

In the past, when I was more self-centered, I needed you to make me feel good about myself. Then, when I grew more open and became more we-centered, I wanted you to join with me as a team, so we could work together and create a good life for ourselves and with our friends. But now I need your love in a different way.

I still enjoy feeling good with myself, with you, and with our friends. But your love invites me beyond my own thoughts and emotions. Your surrender draws me even deeper than all bodies.

Words cannot describe the unbounded place your love illumines. Here, now, deeper than my own heart yet more open then the farthest reaches I can see, your love awakens an openness of bliss.

This bliss isn't different from anything. My feet, your smile, the trees are all made of this bliss, this openness, this love. There are no words for that which is not other than any thing, and yet opens deeper than everything, and spreads wider than all. This openness is where your love invites me to awaken. I long to ravish you open to God here. This is the openness we are born of and the openness we die into. This is the love that our two bodies remember through their embrace when we allow our yearning to open without end.

If you have a more feminine sexual essence, your *strength* is your devotional capacity to open to God in two-bodied form. Yearning open with your lover, you become *two* who open as one love.

Rather than only being responsible for your own body to open, you become responsible first for opening as love through two bodies with your lover, then for opening as love through all bodies. Love is openness. This openness yearns at the heart of everyone. Through two-bodied practice, you learn to feel and breathe this yearning at everybody's heart and surrender open as the love that lives the universe.

While making love, you and your man practice opening beyond self-enclosure. Your surrendered yearning draws your man beyond his fearful shells, into you, deeply into your body and heart. He yields his last hold of separation and enters fully into your love, guiding your surrender even as he dissolves with you, opening as one love.

As one love passionately emerging through two bodies, your pleasure is a deep unfolding, wave upon wave of ever deepening surrender, opening out—not to your man, since your man and you are unseparate, but opening out deeper than your yearning and wider than the skies, without end. His love, your love, is aflame from source to endless openness. Your bodies and hearts surrender open to feel and breathe the openness of all hearts, even as orgasmic waves of unbearable bliss continue carrying love wider open.

For days after such lovemaking, your body reverberates with love's resonance. Your womb is relaxed and full. Your face is soft and bright. Your heart is relaxed open, unshelled, and so you can feel and breathe the love at the heart of everyone.

Together, in two-bodied devotion, you and your man can often open more deeply than your individual habits otherwise allow. Your love demands his, and his love demands yours. Your feminine heart can offer a devotional openness so inviting that your lover has no choice but to come to full presence through his fear and numbness and enter you with utter integrity. His fully present masculine heart can claim you so deeply that you have no choice but to open and surrender as love's bliss, larger than you would ever do on your own.

Your man's body of love is a wedge that can open you to God. Your man's heart is a force that can claim you beyond your self-centered moods. Learning to open with your man prepares you to open in loving communion with everyone's heart.

As you learn to open with your lover in two-bodied embrace and breathe as one heart, you begin to feel all bodies as your body, all hearts as one heart. Sitting in a room with five friends, you feel and breathe their needs, their tensions, their suffering, and the love that yearns to open through their hearts and bodies. You are naturally moved to serve their openness with yours.

You are not weak for wanting to be claimed open by your lover; you are simply feeling your deepest truth—your heart is here to be claimed by all, offered to all as love's fullest light and most tender openness of yearning.

Nevertheless, because all bodies die, your intimate relationship is tinged by sadness. Your man will eventually leave you, betray you, ignore you, or die. One way or another, his personal presence will no longer give you what your heart desires most. At some point, you will lose your beloved. Your two-bodied practice of love is therefore offered through a heart raw with love's impending loss.

Your heart can remain vulnerable and open, willing to suffer the absence of your beloved's presence without closing and pouting like a child. Spiritual and sexual maturity require that you develop the capacity to feel your heart's deepest yearning moment by moment, whether or not you are with a lover. Are you allowing yourself to yearn open right now so you can feel your heart's most divine depth of love? Can you trust your heart's yearning, softening just as you are, so you can breathe and feel everyone's heart while giving your love to all?

Your man is a temporary blessing of divine presence, a form of grace. Love's force is given to you through the form of man, so you can practice breathing and feeling love deep in your yearning heart as you offer your *whole body* to be opened by love and given as love's gift.

Even now, in this moment, with or without a man, you can practice breathing deeply and fully. You can feel everyone from your heart and breathe their hearts in and out of yours, and you can practice relaxing your whole body so love can have its way through you.

Especially, the more feminine parts of your body—the places where you feel the most yearning to be touched, entered, caressed, or ravished—those are the parts to practice relaxing open. Your neck, your breasts, your belly, your vagina, your hips, your buttocks, your legs, your feet—open your entire body and especially the most yearning and responsive parts.

Dear Lover

By relaxing your body and breathing love-energy in and out of every part, your tension eases open and love can flow more fully through you.

You may choose to practice dancing, yoga, or even masturbating as an exercise to help open your heart and body to the flow of love. While you practice your chosen discipline or art of whole-body surrender, always remember to breathe love in and out of your heart, in and out of your entire body, through every pore.

You can allow your body and heart to surrender open so large that you feel and breathe the openness or love that yearns at the heart of everyone. You can magnify your pleasure until your body and heart are forced to open more. Feel how deeply you want to be claimed and taken by love, and how deeply you want to surrender open and offer yourself to be taken.

Your man probably feels your heart mostly through the openness of your body, especially through your offering of sexual devotion. With a wounded heart, even though you have been betrayed in the past and will be again, you can practice to feel and breathe open, alive as love's yearning. While making love through two bodies, you can practice receiving your man's penetration so deeply no part of your heart or body is left untaken by love. And you can practice all day, feeling and breathing the yearning at everyone's heart, while opening your body to be taken by love just as fully.

12.

Loving Larger
Than Fear

Until I met you, I was waiting for a woman with whom I could open completely. I wanted a woman who would not settle for less than love's fullness, from me or from her. And if I did settle for less, I wanted a woman who would let me know.

But I have grown in my capacity to open to God, and I want to open with you, now, dear lover. I am ready for your trust. I commit to trusting the depth of your love, even though I know that sometimes you will close. Still, I trust the depth of your love. I trust your commitment to love. And I want you to trust mine.

I need your heart's sensitive response so I can navigate our opening together with your heart's intuition. I also need you to trust my commitment and capacity to navigate our hearts open *to God. If you don't trust my navigation, I'd rather you weren't with me. I'd rather that you were with another man who you could genuinely trust to open you. I don't want to suffer your mistrust—I'd rather be alone, or with a woman who inspired and trusted my capacity to lead our dance open in bliss. I want to be with a woman who trusts me enough to surrender open to God with me.*

If you don't trust my capacity to navigate us open in communion with your heart, then leave me, and find a man worthy of your trust. But if I do open you more deeply than you have opened yourself, then give yourself to me, entrust your heart to me, so I may open you and be invited beyond my own hesitancy by the depth of your love and the strength of your yearning.

I f your heart's hurt causes you to close or protect yourself, then you are no longer able to receive your man's presence—or the divine presence for which he provides the wedge. Unentered and unclaimed, you feel empty and frustrated inside. You try to fill the hole of your yearning. You eat, work, shop, chat, and try to satisfy your craving with superficial sex or sweets. The power of your heart's yearning becomes blocked behind shells of fear, so you settle for less than your heart's deepest desire to give and receive love.

Your yearning is either genuinely deep or you are settling for something that can't truly fulfill you. As long as you are willing to settle—for a good but not a great man, for a career and nice vacations, for new furniture and fancy restaurants—you will never be willing to suffer the vulnerable depth that is required for your heart to reach open to be taken by love's divine presence.

What you settle for is determined by your fear.

You may be afraid to be without a man's support, so you settle for the man who has loved you the deepest so far. His love may not be unwavering. His integrity may be slipshod. His commitment may be ambiguous. But he says he loves you, you love him, and you do share some moments of great beauty.

So, you settle for a mediocre relationship because you are *afraid to be alone.* You fill your heart's yearning with an adequate, but not absolutely trustable, man.

As you grow beyond being dependent on a man, you may choose to settle for an independent life because you are *afraid to rely on a man's support.*

You may choose to live alone, or perhaps you live your independence in a so-called "self-responsible" relationship based on "equality" with a man who gives you the space to do what you want and take care of yourself.

Such a man is safe; you know he won't physically hurt you and he shares his feelings with you in a sensitive way. But still, you wouldn't trust him with your total heart-surrender. You can't give yourself to him entirely, because he doesn't have the depth to know you fully and open you to God. He is a good partner, perhaps, for raising children and creating a comfortable household, but he rarely shocks you open to God in love's ravishment.

He is not dangerous enough to swoon you. He is not certain enough of his own purpose to take you open in utter confidence. He is a good man, but not a great man. You are afraid of losing the security and comfort you have acquired, and so you settle for the benefits of living with a man who respects you and cooperates with your plans. You know there is more to life, your heart yearns for deeper surrender, but you will hardly even admit to yourself how badly you want to be claimed by a force stronger than yourself, taken open in love beyond your own resistance, ravished open in an ecstasy more heart-true than the comfort of your safe arrangements.

Finally, you grow beyond fearful independence. You are no longer afraid to confess that you want a man who you trust to open your heart more than yourself. Your heart yearns to be taken open by a man whose depth and integrity guide your heart open *better* than you can guide yourself. You realize that you are not weak; you can guide your life—financially, socially, artistically—just fine. But this kind of self-guidance at the surface of your life is not your deepest pleasure. Navigating your own heart's openness doesn't allow the ecstatic surrender for which your heart yearns.

As successful as you may be in your life, you long to merge with a man who can take you open beyond your shells by his deep and authentic claim, his gentle but persistent command—the dangerous demand of a man who will not settle for anything less than your total heart-giving.

He is willing to violate you open into God, to enter your resistance with a smile, to coax your heart from beyond crossed arms, to ravish you open—especially when your habits of fear and childish pout would keep you closed. He is not to be trusted to give you space, but you can trust that he will not be derailed by your resistance. His train is going straight open to where you want to go, and he embraces your refusal with the same humor and impeccable insistence with which he embraces all of life's changes.

He takes you, relentlessly, humorously, unflinchingly, where your deep heart most yearns to open, and he does not take your resistance seriously. You want more space? You want to be left alone to sulk in moods of closure? You've got the wrong man. Your man can guide your heart open more surely than you can, and you know it. Your refusal is only a moment of drama; you know, sooner or later, your pleasure is to surrender to the surety of his loving command.

Eventually, you are only willing to settle for a man whose heart-opening guidance you trust *more than yours*. You are only willing to settle for a man to whom you can surrender, knowing that through his sure claim, divine love guides you open more deeply and consistently than you have been able to open yourself. Your loving has grown large enough to encompass worship in the form of two bodies.

Your knowledge of love is larger than a self-guided woman's fear. You know that nothing is lost—and divine fullness is gained—by offering your superior devotional love-light to a man who offers you his superior heart-ravishment, so together you both open more fully and consistently than either of you tend to open on your own. Openness is love. This same love yearns open at everyone's heart. Your *commitment* to open to God through two-bodied form prepares you to open as this love alive at the heart of all bodies.

13.

Trusting Your Man
to Open You

Dear lover, you have told me about the men you have been with in the past. You have told me why you left them, or why they left you. Hearing you talk of some of them, I can understand your mistrust of men. I can understand why you sometimes hold your love back from me and don't trust to surrender your heart and body wide open to me.

But I also wonder, why did you choose me if you really don't trust me? Or, is your mistrust just residue of tension from your past? Why did you choose those other men in your life, the men who in the past have failed, in one way or another, to allow you to surrender your yearning open as love's offering without the tension of mistrust?

You have told me how deeply you long to surrender open with a man you can trust. I hope I can be that man. I will practice with you so our loving continues to deepen beyond our remaining fear. But even as we practice opening together, I sometimes feel you closing to me and I wonder, are you choosing to stay with me even though you don't trust me to open you to God?

Your lover is with you for the sake of love; he wants you to receive his masculine love and he wants to receive your feminine love. He wants you to trust his gift of heart-direction more than your own and you want him to value your gift of heart-light more than his own—it would disturb you if he spent more hours looking in the mirror admiring his own body's shine than yours.

You want him to notice—in fact, worship—your body's radiant beauty and your heart's light of divine love and he wants you to acknowledge and worship his heart's capacity to spiritually and sexually ravish you open to God. This two-bodied devotion only works when two bodies are better than one; when you are opened more by his deep command and heart-guidance than by your own efforts, and he is opened more by being drawn into your heart of devotion more deeply than his self-enclosure would otherwise allow him.

If you don't trust your man's capacity to take you open where you want to go spiritually and sexually—*more than you trust your own*—then you won't open fully with him, nor should you. If he is more committed to attending to his own radiance than yours, and you are more committed to surrendering to your own heart's direction rather than his, you are both still too self-involved to offer your deepest gifts and open without bounds.

Your independence will evoke his independence: he will find ways to receive feminine radiance without you. He will spend time in nature's radiance—surfing, hiking, skiing—or he'll choose to relax with the energy of music or a soothing beer rather than with your untrusting heart.

Due to your shells of mistrust, you may have chosen a man who *can't* guide your body and heart open to God better than you, directing your life so love's fullness flows unimpeded. Maybe you *are* better at opening yourself than he is at opening you. If so, you are better off trusting your self-guidance than his.

But if you are with such a man, you have *chosen* him. You have probably come to mistrust external masculine guidance—perhaps you inherited such mistrust from your experience with your parents or past intimate betrayal—and so you have chosen a man who justifies your fearful need to direct your own life.

Your man will feel your lack of trust and you will feel the weakness of his loving command in your life. You can love each other as two independent and self-responsible people, but you will never surrender open in love's most blissful dissolution and he will never commit himself completely in his claim of your heart. You would do better to stay in a safe relationship of two self-reliant and autonomous people than to fake devotion to a man's direction that you do not trust more than yours.

But if you are ready to live a love larger than one body, if you are ready to trust a man's deep presence to wedge you open so the flow of love can open your boundaries beyond self-centered moods of protection, then you are ready to practice the art of *fully* offering your feminine gifts, and thereby fully reciprocating your lover's masculine gifts. Your heart-offered devotion inspires his deep consciousness to open through his fears more than he would open by himself.

You always attract your reciprocal. A woman who worships a man's depth of masculine consciousness attracts and inspires a man who worships her heart of devotional feminine radiance. The openness you induce in one another through your worship expands your capacity to love far beyond each of your bodies, beyond even your two-bodied ecstasy, unfolding your love outward to infinity, feeling every heart's yearning, breathing open wider than the moon and sun and stars. Your sexual embrace can open you to God through the loving worship of masculine consciousness and feminine light.

14.

You Attract
Your Reciprocal

When I feel the openness of your heart, I can feel how closed I have been to love. The softness of your body invites me to relax open and feel you. And when I feel you, the depth of your yearning calls the depth of my desire for you. I want to enter you as deeply and passionately as I feel your heart yearning to be entered, and I want to open you even more deeply with my love.

But when your yearning heart is hidden behind the tense cover of your body, then it is easy for me to continue on my way, doing my duties, accomplishing my tasks, or resting alone, without you. I can't fully see your heart's light through the hardness of your demeanor. I can't really feel your heart's longing for love, only *your desire to get something done. I assume you want to be left alone to do what you need to do. So, I don't touch your hurried body or infiltrate your shell of doing with my love.*

I have learned that sometimes, even though you don't show it, your heart actually does want to be touched by my love beneath your headlong actions. So, I have learned to take a moment and slow down with you when the time feels right, pressing my love into you, until you soften and open your heart, before continuing with your day. And you have learned to do the same for me, dear lover.

But I wonder if you are aware of how significantly your current disposition affects my heart's desire to enter you and my body's desire to touch you in love. Your yearning heart opens a love-depth in my otherwise surface day and calls me to feel into your deep longing, inviting my desire to open with you as love's surrender.

But if I am only able to feel your tense body, then your company feels more like stress that I have to deal with. Although I am committed to opening you as deeply as I can with my love even when you are closed, the depth of my passionate desire for you is invited by the fullness of your yearning, which you show, moment

by moment, through the trusting surrender of
your body's openness to love.

I f you don't have a man in your life who claims your heart with his love and opens you to God, you are probably not fully offering your heart to be claimed while opening your body to flow with love's bliss—right now. You always attract and inspire a man as deeply committed to opening in love as you are—right now—which means that a man will be as actively present with you as you are actively radiating your love and allowing your yearning to open in his company and when you are alone.

Right now, how fully is your heart yearning open? How deeply do you want your heart's longing to be met? How actively are you allowing love's yearning to open through your feet, your thighs, your neck? Are your heart and belly as open now as if you were making love with a trusted lover while breathing the hearts of all beings? Probably not. Most likely, your heart is less than devotionally surrendered and your body is less than overflowing with love's yearning pleasure. Therefore, you will attract a man who is less present than your heart truly desires.

Deep in your heart, you probably want to be with a man who could be *totally* present with you when you are together, as if he were making love with you, even at the dinner table or while taking a walk. To attract such a man, to evoke his fullness, you must be offering yours. His presence and the offering of your heart's yearning go together; he drifts when you close down, you close down when he drifts. He wants to claim you when you trust him with your worship of his consciousness. And you open, offering your yearning and surrender to him, when you feel his deep claim and worship of your heart.

If you are not currently in relationship with such a man, feel yourself: Right now, are you opening and breathing the love that flows at the heart of all beings, feeling their suffering and their joy? Are you actively open-ing, breathing, and receiving this moment's force of love into your body and heart—as if you were taking your lover deep inside, offering him your most vulnerable yearning of feminine devotion and the untamed gifts of your energy?

If you are offering your heart's deepest yearning, then you will attract and inspire a man's deepest presence, right now. If your heart's surrender is cautious and your body's flow of energy is minimal, then you will, in this moment, attract and inspire a man whose presence is easily distracted and whose heart is uncalled to feel you deeply.

How do you open now? Start by breathing deeply, filling your belly pregnant with breath-force while you inhale, then exhaling and releasing all hold of tension. Breathe deeply in and out through every part of your body. Breathe in and out of your feet so your toes wiggle and you continue breathing open every part of your body: your legs come alive, your vagina softens and moistens, your belly grows round and full with pleasure, your heart opens and feels, your arms and hands and fingers unfold as sprouts of your heart, your throat softens and your neck elongates, your face and lips and eyes and head all relax open. Breathe fully and relax your entire body open, from toe to head.

Then, as you breathe, feel outward from your heart. If you have a lover, then breathe him—his shape, his joy, his suffering—in and out of your heart. If you have children, then breathe them and all your friends in and out of your heart. Open your heart to feel your community and eventu-ally the entire world, breathing all—people, animals, plants, ocean, forest, even the night's darkness—in and out of your heart. Allow your heart to open and feel all, breathing all. Feel alive as all, breathing as the yearning that opens at all hearts.

Soften your body so your heart can actively breathe the openness of this moment. This moment *exists* as openness. Feel the actual *aliveness* of this moment, living within you, living as you, and living all around you. This moment is alive as love, as openness.

As if you were soaking in an ocean of love, relax open your throat, heart, belly, and genitals to receive love's saturation. Lovingly melt your heart and body open as the fullness of this moment.

With practice, you learn to breathe and feel the love alive as the universe and the yearning at the heart of all beings. You learn to melt open and receive every moment's love-fullness into your whole body. In response, your natural gesture is to offer yourself open as love, as a lover gives herself to her beloved. It is as if God were making love with you and you were offering all of yourself open to God.

Right now, are you receiving this moment's divine ravishment down to your love-splayed toes? Are you offering your body as a sacred gift, surrendering your deep heart fully to be claimed by love's earthly embodiment?

To attract a man of heart-depth and inspire his fullness, you must be offering yours.

15.

Why Men
Hold Back

⌒

Many times, I have heard you tell me that you can't feel me fully with you, truly seeing you and loving you. But I do love you. I can feel my love for you, and I can feel your love for me.

Yet, I also have to admit that there are times when you seem untrustable to me. You tell me one thing, and then change your mind the next moment. You seem so happy, and then suddenly, for no apparent reason, you seem upset. Sometimes I can stay fully with you while your emotions confound me, but often I pull back.

I wait for you to calm down. Or, I try to talk with you about how you feel so I can understand the problem and deal with it. My attempts to listen to you, however, don't seem to

matter too much, because the same thing hap-
pens again. I lose trust in what you say because
it often seems to change, and I hold back so I
don't get too angry with what I feel are your
groundless words and extreme moods.

Through the years, however, we have grown.
You have learned to allow your deep yearning
to open through all your changing emotions. So
now it is easier for me to feel your true heart's
desire, not just your surface words and changes.
I have learned to really stay in touch and feel
your deepest heart without getting diverted by
what you say or do on the outside.

I practice to feel your deepest yearning and
see your true heart's light while you say and do
everything. Without holding back from you to
find peace in my own distance, I am awed by
the depth of your love. Your fully shown light
awakens my heart to the love shining open as
every moment.

If a man has a masculine essence, then when he feels most deeply into his heart, he discovers a cognizant beingness that is the nature of this present moment. If you want a deep relationship with a man, then it is worth understanding this unchanging and ever-present consciousness, this "home" where a man knows who he truly is.

This deepest place of being is consciousness itself, which is divine love. From this deep place a man witnesses the passing drama of life. Rested open as this unchanging depth of love, your man is "already dead," so he has nothing to gain or lose that will make any fundamental difference. He can give everything to the world and to you without fear and without holding back. He is not repelled or distracted by your emotional wildness and life's turmoil because he stands free in depth, offering his deepest love as the moments come and go.

Most men have yet to feel their deepest heart of free consciousness. They can't feel their deepest purpose, and so they can't offer their deepest gifts of love, to you or the world. To you, these men feel superficial and not so trustable. You cannot feel their deep heart and authentic confidence. You cannot see the vulnerable strength of death in their eyes. Instead, they appear lost in the games and drama of life, unsure and unable to take you to love's depth.

Most men you know probably hold back, from your emotions and from life's chaos. However, some men genuinely *are* involved and at home in life's fullness just as you are.

For instance, some men truly enjoy talking about their emotions with women. Maybe you have been with a man who is really refreshed by having coffee with you, chatting about recipes, new clothing, and stories of their close friends, and sharing a good cry over their relationship. Some men feel at ease while attending to their child's tantrum, answering the ringing telephone, and keeping a conversation going with their visiting friends while also watching their favorite sport on TV.

Almost all men have some capacity to engage life's commotion, sensual hubbub, and your emotional maelstroms. To some extent, most men can enjoy redecorating your home, planning a wedding, or finger-painting at their child's birthday party with 30 boys and girls eating cake and running to and fro.

Even if a man has a masculine essence, he also embodies some amount of *natural feminine energy*. This part of him is genuinely at home in life's ever-changing fullness, just as you are. However, a man may also have a *fear-built feminine shell:* he may occupy his time in conversation and parties because he has lost touch with death's urgency and his heart's deepest purpose.

You can probably feel the difference between a man who is genuinely enjoying a conversation—but who can still ravish you with his deep masculine claim—and a man who is ungrounded in death's authority, and so chats with a pansy smile.

As a man learns to relax his shells and rediscover his depth, he becomes more of a *free man*—identified with the freedom of unchanging consciousness. His heart-authority and love can most deeply claim your heart. Yet, this same man may need to grow in his capacity to engage your emotional storms without turning away to seek his freedom. He can practice to lovingly enter your wildness without flinching by learning to stay in touch with deep consciousness that is ever-present.

However, until he learns to fully relax as this ever-present and unchanging depth of freedom, he may try to create pseudo-freedom by avoiding, controlling, or suppressing life—and the emotional part of you—that he feels is a potential distraction or entanglement.

A man may hold back from the fracas of relationship and life by focusing on the unchanging goal of a particular project: cutting the lawn, washing his car, playing the stock market, building a house, or writing a book. He may induce pseudo-freedom by drinking a beer, kicking back, and watching TV. He may avoid emotional hubbub by closing himself in his office and gazing steadily into his computer. He may make a genuine attempt to ground himself in the depth of consciousness by eliminating life's entanglements and entering a month-long silent meditation retreat in an effort to achieve "ego death."

You may feel like your man is rejecting you, but he is simply not at home in change and emotional flow like you are. He can handle your emotional expression for a while, but he can't help trying to "fix" you as if your emotional flow were a problem. He tries to resolve your discussions so they are finished, done, and he can get back to no-problem or calm harmony and peace. He often tries to resolve your somethingness into nothingness, steering sexual fullness toward ejaculative emptiness, trying to find a solution to your emotional flow or spiritual suffering so the "problem" is over.

Rather than connecting and sharing a broad emotional flow or enjoying an open-ended dance with your feelings, most men, most often, spend their time suspended in the pseudo-freedom of zoning out in front of a TV, obliterating themselves on drugs, or becoming absorbed in a singular challenge—business deals, rock climbing, studying philosophy—especially those challenges that promise a taste of release or "death."

Most men choose to spend much of their day trying to make a financial "killing," struggling for political freedom, seeking a creative release, an intellectual ah-hah, or spiritual liberation. And, if nothing else, they can watch sports—men at the edge of "death" in a boxing ring or absorbed in the challenge of carrying, kicking, or hitting a ball across a line, whooping in the freedom of a victory.

Even though your man may truly love you and want to spend his life with you, he can often find your emotional flow meaningless and taxing, since your ever-changing energy is so foreign to the freedom of release he seeks: the "final" or changeless consciousness and peace that feels most "home" to his masculine essence. To him, you may always seem to be changing your mind, changing your emotions, loving him, hating him, closing down, and opening up. He knows by now that whatever he does with you today won't make a difference by tomorrow, so he'd often rather invest his time in something that at least has the appearance of achieving some form of freedom or completion.

Unless your deep heart is actively seducing and inspiring your man's deep and fearless consciousness into life, then your native emotional flow may be actively repelling him—even if he genuinely loves you. Until he opens to the freedom of deep consciousness, his greatest fear is losing his tenuously acquired pseudo-freedom by becoming entangled in what seem to be the constraints of life or you, including your love.

He may be afraid to commit to you because he fears losing "other options," even if he loves you. He may pull back after especially deep lovemaking because he is afraid of losing his freedom to the bond that deeper loving may imply to him.

If your man is still growing to feel the freedom inherent in every moment's depth of consciousness, then you will probably have to invite his depth of presence with your depth of love. Your deepest light and heart's yearning can actively invite his depth, seducing or enchanting his deep presence into the dance of relationship and life. Otherwise, he may tend to engage only shallowly, or withdraw in the pseudo-freedom of holding back.

If you want to inspire your man's depth of presence and commitment, offer him your feminine heart's most deep yearning, sexually, actively, and devotionally, receiving him into you completely and responding with full pleasure and trust. If you don't offer him your fullness, then he may never have the opportunity to learn how to enter the feminine heart's deepest demand for love. When he takes time off from his search for pseudo-freedom, his desire to enjoy the feminine may remain shallow. He may go to less "entrapping" feminine sources with which to merge—oceans, forests, music, beer, pornography, or less challenging women.

The *fullness* of your offering of light through your body and heart's yearning—sexually and in every way—attracts and inspires the *depth* of your man's consciousness to enter you and the world.

Your fullest form of inspiration is worship. You can actually worship the depth of your man's consciousness. Even if he is holding back, you can feel the deep part of his heart that you do trust. You can see it deep in his eyes and feel it deep in his heart. His deep consciousness becomes the subject of your devotion, whom you dance for and inspire. You know this fearless presence at his depth, even if he is unable to feel it for himself in the moment.

By reflecting and offering your worship of this deep part of your man's heart, you can help him feel and reclaim his own truth. Your worship of his depth inspires him to feel the free consciousness that he is, at depth. When he can feel and relax open as his deepest heart's freedom, then he not only tolerates your chaos or enjoys conversing with you, he actually worships the depth of your heart's longing and light.

As your mutual worship deepens, your love is lived with humor. Your man pulls away and you smile, knowing the power of your heart to seduce him back into you and life. You close down or erupt emotionally and he smiles, knowing the power of his presence to penetrate your resistant energy and open you to God.

Your feminine fullness of heart yearning will always attract and inspire a reciprocal *depth* of masculine consciousness in your man. If you shirk the depth of your shine, you'll attract a man who hides in isolation, or absorbs his awareness in heartless goals of athletic, financial, or so-called spiritual challenge, or goes to easy sex for shallow pleasure.

Your man prefers that you would simply open without moods of resistance. You prefer that your man would simply desire you without requiring your active enchantment. He is often too tired to want to deal with your emotional concerns. You are often too stressed or exhausted to want to "put it out" and attract him.

You can each complain: You want more of his loving presence and he wants more sexual energy from you. You can each compromise: He pretends to be interested in what you have to say and you pretend to enjoy his clumsy gropes and superficial life.

Or, you can each devote yourself to enjoying your heart's *deepest* desire. Your man can relax open and "die" as the deep consciousness that is the source of this moment, free to give his fullest love to you and all without holding back. And you can relax open and love yourself, your man, and the entire world, so that your heart's light opens wide as this moment's livingness. Through this mutual offering, you and your man can inspire and invite the deepest gifts of each other's heart.

16.

Your Force
of Attraction

❧

Dear lover, you don't hide your sexual charms
from me—you know how to turn me on more
than anyone ever has—but you don't settle for
mere genital friction and affectionate embrace.
Your heart's deep longing draws me beyond the
pursuit of pleasure—beyond the pursuit of
anything.

The love that shows through the openness of
your yearning awakens me, here and now, to
the love that shines open as this moment. Your
love inspires my deepest gifts to flow spontaneously from my heart to everyone.

But sometimes you offer me your love and
I can't open to meet your heart. My mind is
occupied with plans or my body is running on
stress. Even when you massage me lovingly or

speak to me in sweet tones of honey, I still can't open fully with you.

During these times when I lack the ability to love you as deeply as you are loving me, I am astonished by your openness. Sometimes you cry, and my heart melts. At other times, you simply look into my eyes inviting me, your body soft and your heart open, even though my unlove is hurting you. I can feel how resistant I am in comparison to your offering of love's openness. Your love is so strong, vulnerable, and infinite.

Your choice to stay open when I am closed gives me an opportunity to open with you. When I am already indisposed to love, your clo- sure would push me away even further. But your choice to stay open while showing me your hurt and your heart's longing for my love gives me a chance to meet your open heart with mine.

Your attractive power is unequalled. Feminine energy is the most attractive force on earth. And, to many men, your feminine *sexual* energy is what they find most irresistible.

You know that you can wrap a man around your little finger by offering your feminine sexual energy and attracting him into your field of influence. You can use this power for your own sake, to get what you want from a man. You can also minimize your attractive power because you feel it isn't fair to manipulate a man; you may feel that each person is self-responsible, and that you should be able to get what you want in your life by using your own masculine direction rather than by attracting a man into doing what you want.

However, when your love grows wide open, you can use your irresistible power of attraction for the sake of magnifying the love alive at the heart of all beings.

Yes, you can get a man to do just about anything, and you know it. So, what are you going to attract him into doing? Buying you a nice house? Giving you the space to guide your own life? Or, offering his deepest gifts to you and all beings while opening his heart to God?

Are you a selfish witch, a self-sufficient witch, or a witch for the sake of drawing your man and all beings open as a gift for all?

You may be afraid of your own power of attraction and influence. You may be afraid of living open beyond your single-bodied form. So your yearning and capacity to love, your ability to attract all into love's communion, may lie latent and buried beneath layers of fearful shells.

Whether you are with a man or not, you can open and offer the attractive power of your feminine sexual energy *from your deepest heart* for the sake of all beings—and by doing so, you will attract a deep man into your life. And if you are already with a man, instead of waiting for his integrity to deepen, you can open right now and elicit your man's depth with the openness of your love's yearning. You can offer your depth of heart right now and attract from your man his reciprocal depth of presence.

Something as simple as the way you pour a cup of tea, for instance, can awaken your man's deepest heart. You can walk across the kitchen floor, moving like a dancer, an overjoyed lover, a woman whose womb is full of pleasure and whose limbs are gliding with love. As you pour the tea, you can feel the liquid filling your man's cup as your love would fill his life. You can gaze into his eyes, offering your deepest heart through your yearning.

If his casual non-presence persists, you need not cater to his superficiality. You stand in place, yearning wide open as love—not tense or needy, but as a work of art, fully aware of your radiant gifts, offering your heart's beauty through your poise and grace—until he notices. You can break the pattern of casual mistreatment by *demanding* his worship—without saying a word, simply by offering the depth of your heart's yearning and the strong flow of love through your bodily grace and poise. If you are steady and strong in your offering, he cannot resist.

The seductive light in your eyes, the tilt of your hips, the clothes you wear, the beauty with which you move and show your feminine form—your gifts of radiance are irresistible to your man. He may try to persist in non-presence—reading magazines, talking about stupid things—but if you don't buy into your own pain of rejection, and if you maintain your fullness without catering to his pipsqueak style of shallow attention, then his thin spell will be broken.

Your artful offering of love's yearning evokes his depth. The persistence of your heart's light evokes the stability of his presence. Your graceful dance—simply the way you walk, move your fingers, and turn your head—can evoke his attention and awe.

Offering your deepest yearning and love is an art that will attract and inspire your man's deepest presence, even when you feel tired or not in the mood. If you chat about your day while trudging across the kitchen floor, casually pouring some tea and plopping down on your chair with a furrowed brow and frumpy posture, you are empowering your man's non-presence. You are actually enforcing habits of non-communion. He is unattracted, unevoked from his newspaper-zone of nothingness.

But if you *practice* opening so your body is breathing love's fullness—as if you were on the verge of the most loving orgasm you could imagine—he will notice. If your hips are moving with the same pleasure as if you were dancing to your favorite music, his attention will move to your body. If your eyes are soft with love's yearning, if your voice is spoken as if in bed, modulated by the tone of love's pleasure, his newspaper-world will feel paltry.

Remember, he is not at home in life as fully as you are. His basic orientation is toward the freedom of empty and unchanging consciousness. If his alternative to this freedom of emptiness is your clumsy body, your harping voice, your emotional neediness, or your habitual talk, he will learn to tune you out. If, however, the sound of your voice feels like the most loving sexual moan, if the movement of your body looks like a dancer gliding with ecstasy, if your speech and facial expression are of love, yearning, and worship, he will do anything for you.

In your moments of emphasizing self-reliance, you may negate the radiant power of your feminine attraction and try to emphasize your worldly functionality and intellectual capacity. Your sexuality seems to be only a small part of who you are as a "whole person." Offering your sexual enchantment to awaken your man's presence feels like a diminishment of your wholeness and a cheap manipulation of his desire—*because you stop short of attracting his attention open to God's fullness through your sexuality.*

When your love deepens, you feel your sexuality as a potent form of divine art, quite likely the most attractive gift you can offer to your man, your most direct way to invite him open into God through love. You give your heart's yearning and your body's form as a divine offering of love. You seduce your man not only to your surface, but to your depth.

You will attract in a man, and evoke in your man, the depth of worship corresponding to your offering. If you want your man to treat you like a scheming vamp, then offer your superficial charms to manipulate his superficial desires. If you want your man to treat you like a colleague and friend, then offer your humor, knowledge, and talents to interest him. If you want your man to worship your love as his chosen source of divine feminine radiance, then offer him your fullest sexual art of devotional surrender—through every gesture, movement, sound, and expression. Offer your yearning and devotion to God through the God in him.

And even if you don't have a man, why would you want to live a life that was less than devotional art? For your own sake, for the sake of all beings, for God's sake, wouldn't you rather relax open as love's offering than contract in stress and subjective confusion? Even if you were cooking dinner for yourself, alone in your house, why move as less than love's open dance while offering your heart's yearning brighter than the sun shines? You can open as pleasure, move as a goddess, wash soapsuds off your dishes as if making exquisite love—you can live open as love's art, moving in every aspect of life as a reflection of the sacred.

You are either allowing your life to be lived open as love, or you are settling for less. You are either disciplining your body to open as love's art, or you are encasing your heart in shells of habit. For instance, sheer habit determines the tone of voice you would use to ask your man, "Would you like some tea?"

You can change your act into art. Rather than acting from habit, you can practice acting as an artful offering that will evoke the depth of your man's heart and fill his life with light. Imagine you were about to have an orgasm of the deepest kind, so your heart and body were surrendered open like an infinite flower of pleasure. Now, with what tone would your words emerge from the womb of your pleasure, "Would you like some tea?"

You can speak, move, and breathe as acts of habit, or as offerings of art. You can feel and offer your whole body as a gift of love's beauty, showing the light of your deepest heart. As love yearns open through your body of devotional surrender, you will naturally evoke adoration, reverence, and deep heart-communion. This is your moment-by-moment *choice:* to act as a habitual personality, or to offer your life as art, moving as love's sacred gift.

Your life reflects the sacred as fully as you are willing to feel and express your heart and body's *deepest* desires. For instance, when your body is touched, for what do you most deeply yearn?

Feel the soft surface of your skin. Would you like to be stroked so that shivers of pleasure run through your body? Do you desire to be caressed so that your heart opens deeper, evoking tears of vulnerable surrender? What kind of touch would unfold the very deepest core of your heart's yearning, perhaps hidden and unexpressed your entire life?

Being touched can feel good. But being touched can also open your deepest heart. What kind of touch do you usually settle for? With what depth of yearning are you willing to offer your skin to be touched?

The depth of your heart's yearning—offered through your skin, voice, and movement—attracts and inspires a man whose offering to you and the world is equally heart-deep. Even your friends and children are inspired to express more deeply their divine gifts when you allow your deepest yearning to unfold.

Love's true offering emerges from your deepest yearning as various desires simultaneously occupy your heart. You probably desire ice cream on occasion, but the flush of yum is brief. Raising a family can occupy you for years, but how many mothers do you know whose children are grown and gone and whose once-occupied heart now feels empty and seeks solace in a lonely house? You may long for many pleasures in life, some more shallow and some quite deep. But for your heart to enjoy true and lasting fulfillment, you can learn to feel and offer your *deepest* yearning in every moment, through every desire, throughout your life.

What does it feel like to offer your deepest desire through your whole body? Imagine, right now, you were with a truly trustable lover. His body presses against yours, flesh to soft flesh. He feels any resistance you may have, and he opens through it. He breathes with you, feeling your every move and need. Your arm moves an inch, and he grasps your wrist, drawing your arms above your head, pinning you down, opening you.

When you need a rest he stops; when you need more force he enters you with passion. Because you trust him, you can relax open with him. You allow him more deeply inside of you, in your body and heart. His loving opens you more, and soon your invitation grows strong. Your body and heart open to take his love deeper, filling you more than you can take without surrendering. All your boundaries dissolve as you receive his love without fear or resistance, until you are gone open, he is gone open, and love moves open as all.

Enraptured in love's deepest bliss, how would your tongue and jaw feel? How would your pelvis ease? How would your throat feel? What tones would your vocal cords offer? How would your hand brush away the hair falling in your face? Would your belly be hard or soft? Would you have limp ankles or happy feet? What happens to your breathing when you feel this depth of love, even in your imagination? How would you live and move right now if you were open in the fullest loving you can imagine?

Right now, the only way you can know that you are *not* being fully loved is because you can intuit how it would feel to *be* fully loved. The only way you know that you are not open in divine bliss is because you can intuit a way of opening that is more divine, more blissful, than you are allowing yourself to open now.

You *already* intuit your deepest divine love and gifts, right now. If you didn't, you wouldn't yearn as you do. You may not be able to put words on your feeling, but you can intuitively feel deeper and deeper into the hole of your yearning. You can open and express this love spontaneously from your deepest heart through your whole body, so every movement of your life is a reflection of the sacred.

Sometimes your own body and mind won't be able to sustain the openness necessary for your deepest heart to be offered. Your attention, and thus your energy, will go to superficial pleasures, sweet foods and nice caresses. You can intuit a much deeper yearning, but you may settle for less.

Also, those around you may not be able to handle the inherent demand of your deepest offering. Many people are afraid of opening, so you will frequently be met by their closure.

Therefore, your deepest heart will want more love than you or others seem capable of sustaining. You may constantly wish you were able to give and receive more love—and that your lover were more capable, too.

How you respond to your heart's wish for love depends on how deeply you are willing to feel and express your yearning without closing. Are you being a needy woman, grasping for security by manipulating others with your superficial charms? Are you being a hardened and independent-acting woman, suppressing your irresistible shine and keeping your heart unsurrendered despite your love's aching? Or, are you being a divine offering of love, gracefully articulating love's *deepest* light and yearning through your unique art of feminine devotion, offering your love even through a heart that may be open and hurting?

Offer your feminine sexual energy through your deepest heart's yearning. The radiance of your deep heart's yearning is the beacon that attracts men of integrity. Not your neediness. Not your independence. Rather, deep men are attracted and inspired by your heart's acheful offering, your blissfully anguished heart-plea to be taken—and the fact that your heart's light won't settle for anything less than total claim in divine love.

Throughout your life, continue to intuit and offer your heart's deepest longing, while you are touched sublimely and callously, while your children come and go, while your lover withdraws from you and while he shares your heart's openness.

The light of your heart's deepest longing, offered through your whole body, is your deepest force of attraction. Your surrender and offering of love's divine light is also the source of your life's art, your devotional gift to all beings, and the only way to live open as your heart's deepest pleasure.

Would you rather live any other way?

17.

Your Man Is
Your Choice

Dear lover, I don't want you to give up. I know the men in your past have hurt you and that sometimes I am unable to meet you. But please don't settle for less than your heart's most deep desire. I have seen so many women give up and settle for a mediocre relationship that doesn't open them to God. I have also seen women try to bypass the often difficult practice of two-bodied devotion by trying to love themselves.

These women learn that by loving themselves just as they are, and by loving their man even with all his human limits, then they can feel OK. They can feel warmly OK with their own humanness and their man's. They don't need things to be perfect anymore. They are able to love and accept things as they are.

But I would be disappointed if you settled for this. Loving you and me as we are—loving your own shells and loving me even with all my imperfections—is a first step. Yet a greater gift is allowing your heart's deepest expression to illuminate my life so I can see more than I can by myself. And if you will choose me—or another man—who you trust to open your heart deeper than you can by loving your own human limits and shells, then your heart will flower far beyond simple OK-ness with the way things are.

The first step is to love yourself, me, and everyone with all of our imperfections; we are divine and OK just as we are. The next step is to open in the fuller illumination of two-bodied devotional trust. Then, we can see more and offer our love more profoundly than we could without each other's loving reflection and heart-demand. Yet another step in love's flowering is to trust and open fully as the love that yearns to shine through the hearts of all beings.

In bed, you may enjoy taking charge, teaching, and leading your lover on occasion, but if your man is inadequate—if your spiritual and sexual guidance is *necessary* because your man's capacity to navigate is untrustworthy—then you remain unsurrendered, and your body accumulates discontent in the form of tension, stress, exhaustion, or depression. You want your man to know you and reach you; you want him to know your body and how to bloom your openness.

If your man's depth isn't sufficient to feel you and open you, then your body becomes edgy, your voice sharp, your movements ungraceful. Your belly is not full with pleasure. Why? Because as much as you may genuinely enjoy guiding your own life professionally, artistically, or politically, your feminine essence yearns to surrender as all love rather than maintain control and make all the decisions *spiritually* and *sexually*.

Have you ever leaned into a man's loving guidance? Have you relinquished control and allowed your sweetly surrendered heart to flow open like the ocean, wild and deep, rather than holding the narrow direction of a functional canal? Spiritually and sexually, your heart wants to be entered and inhabited by deep love and impeccable integrity. You want to swoon as love's fullest offering without always having to initiate the lead and guide your lover.

You may not mind managing the 100 employees at your corporation, but your heart finds little pleasure in managing your man. As a human functionary—a businesswoman, a professional artist, a mother, a politician—you may genuinely love to be in charge. But if you have a feminine essence, then when it comes time to open in spiritual and sexual intimacy with your lover, you wish you didn't have to always be in charge, telling your man what to do, directing him into greater depth, teaching him how to open. You want to offer yourself open without always having to initiate and lead.

Your heart longs to be felt, known, entered, loved, and commanded open, yet you may also be afraid to trust.

Every man has his limits, so you may be afraid to receive command from your man, knowing he may falter, seeing that he *does* falter at times. Your man may lack intellectual capacity. Or he may be energetically insensitive. Your man may be clumsy, hesitant, or too safe and unadventurous. Your man may lack the depth, force, and gentle insistence necessary to earn your surrender. If you don't totally trust your man's command sexually and spiritually, *then you have chosen him so that you do not have to surrender open, offering your heart's deepest yearning.*

If you are with a man you don't trust, it is only because you prefer unsurrendered love to surrendering wide open in total trust. It feels safe. You are afraid to let go of control—part of you doesn't trust love's command—so you have chosen a man who doesn't demand your surrender with his depth of integrity. If you did trust the command of love, you would only settle for a deep man capable of opening you more deeply than you could instruct him.

Men are like trains. They are going somewhere. Choosing and staying with a man is like choosing to get on a train. You will end up going where your man goes, spiritually and sexually, or you will have to get off his train. You cannot change a man's direction to yours without losing trust in his capacity to navigate.

You don't want a rigid man, but you want a man whose heart's courage and authentic truth runs deep. You want a man who feels you, listens to you, considers everything you have said, and then claims you, taking you to where you *couldn't* tell him to take you, even if you tried. He takes your heart to new depths of adventure and openness, and he shows you new aspects of life.

You can—and should—give your man your fullest expression of feeling, offering him your feedback, your love, and your responsive heart's spontaneous expression of pleasure and pain. A really good man will embrace all the feedback and feeling you have offered him, consider everything you have shown him, and then, claiming your heart deeply, he will decide where his train is going, with you or without you. And you want it that way.

You don't want a man who adapts his direction to where you say you want to go. What good is he then? You might as well navigate your own direction if your man changes his path to follow what you tell him. You want to feel and be able to respect his wisdom.

A dependent woman is willing to lose her own strength of direction for the sake of keeping her man's affections and staying on his train, even if she doesn't fully trust her man's spiritual and sexual wisdom. An independent woman insists on equality in the guidance of their shared train, or chooses to guide her own train, which is smart if she doesn't trust her man's capacity to open her spiritually and sexually more than she can open herself.

But a woman ready for opening deeply in two-bodied devotion won't settle for less. She has matured to know the sublime pleasure of surrendering open to be lived as the untamed force of love, so she chooses a man whose command takes her *deeper* and *beyond* where she even trusted was possible.

A deep relationship of intimate communion takes you more open than you could go on your own. If your man isn't capable of commanding you open in blissful and ever-deepening surrender, why did you choose him? Is there a part of you—perhaps a subconscious part—that *chose* him so that you wouldn't have to surrender open in total trust? Is it possible that part of you is afraid to open your heart without protection, so you have attracted and chosen a man whose fear taints his command, justifying your mistrust and closure?

Do you trust your *own* heart's deepest yearning?

If you are genuinely ready to open as unbound love and your man is truly unwilling to grow, then you may have to leave him. If his commitment to growing in spiritual and sexual command is inadequate for your heart to trust, then you may need to move forward without him. Keep your heart open while you suffer the him-shaped void of aloneness until your devotion deepens enough to attract and choose a trustworthy man.

If you really want to surrender open in two-bodied devotional trust, then choose and stay with a man whose train is *already* going deeper and further than you can open yourself.

Choose a man who takes you open more deeply than you have been so far able to take yourself. But also choose a man who takes you deeper than you would go by taking turns navigating, him expecting that you will take charge half the time. A deep man of integrity takes your heart into his heart as he navigates, fine-tuning his actions while feeling your heart's response, always valuing your feedback. But his navigation is not *relinquished* or *weakened* by your feedback or anyone's.

Feeling from his heart outward to all, taking all hearts into account, his actions emerge spontaneously from love's depth, uncurtailed by hesitancy. As he acts, he continually feels your heart and all hearts, fine-tuning every action for the sake of all. You can feel his profound commitment to love and his unconstrained offering of his deepest gifts, so you can relax open and offer *your* heart's deepest gifts. His love-borne command allows your love-borne surrender as well as your fully given feedback.

He offers you his deepest gift by persistently taking you beyond your heart's boundaries into love's fullest surrender and expression. He's opening to God now, with you or without you—and he acknowledges that both of you open more fully as a two-bodied train than alone. Embracing your heart and feeling your exquisite responses, he corrects his errors as he goes without collapsing, his strength of navigation and respect of your feeling-wisdom taking you both open in ever-deepening love and fullness.

If you *don't* want this kind of man, then continue navigating yourself. Show your mistrust in the stressed clench of your belly and the strain of your voice. If you *do* want this kind of man, then practice surrendering open to be commanded by love while fully expressing your heart. If you are alone, then practice feeling your heart and opening your body, breath, and emotions so that love can express through you, unimpeded by your accumulated shells of fear-imposed masculine self-control.

You can go into your room, close the door, take off your clothes and dance to your favorite music. And when you want to stop dancing, keep

Dear Lover

opening. Let love move your limbs and hips, let energy open and express through your pelvis and whole body, especially when you least want to dance. When your mind starts chattering or your body closes down, continue dancing open, practicing to allow the energy of the music to move you more open. Surrender to the divine force flowing through you and express your heart fully through your whole body.

Practice feeling your heart's yearning, softening your muscles, and allowing yourself to be danced as if being inhabited and opened by love's fullest flow. Breathe love in and out of your heart. Feel your friends, your children—feel everyone—and breathe their love in and out of your heart as you dance as big as life. Dance as you breathe everyone. Dancing as everyone, allow your feelings to flow through every cell of your body, crying, screaming, sighing, breathing, and dancing as love expresses through you.

Love is not something that happens or not. Love is a discipline, a constant practice and commitment to feel and *love your shells*, relaxing with humor and surrendering open through your love-softened shells that would otherwise suppress your energy and build walls around your heart.

Love your shells when your fear clamps tight, and then *express your deepest yearning* to your man. If you want a man whose train you trust to take you where you want to go—and beyond—then you can inspire his train with your depth of love's yearning and fine-tune his direction with your heart's intuition and your fullest expression of love's spontaneously offered energy.

If his train is going in the wrong direction, your dance of displeasure gives warning. If his train continues in the wrong direction, your wrath is unmistakable, your fangs growing, your claws emerging, an irrepressible and spontaneous anger dancing through your open heart and body.

You will attract and keep a man who can maintain his integrity with the same consistency that you can offer your dance through love-softened shells without collapse or frustration. And this isn't easy, for either of you.

It is easier for you to give up trying to change your man, learn to love yourself just as you are, and simply grow to tolerate a clod in your house. It is easier for your man to jerk off in the bathroom or find a mistress than to claim you so tenderly and insistently that your surrendered devotion attracts him deeper than tits and ass.

Your man's heart-presence and your heart-devotion must be fully given—fiercely at times, gently at others—or his train will go off track as your offering becomes suppressed or you settle for loving yourself and letting him be as he is. He will veer into the shallows and your unmet heart will eventually become mired in dark moods.

If you want a relationship that reflects the sacred, then, moment by moment, re-feel your deepest heart's yearning. Don't be sidetracked by lesser desires, unless you want to attract and inspire a man equally sidetracked. A man that you choose from your lesser desires may provide security, a family, and fun vacations, but he won't know how to live with you in deep and divine love. By feeling and offering only your lesser desires, you will attract and inspire a man who offers less than your deepest heart wants.

If you want a man who can offer his deepest consciousness and create a sacred relationship with you—perhaps while also providing security, family, and vacations—then feel, trust, and offer your heart's deepest yearning. Then, your love's most divine longing and deepest wisdom will choose the man you truly value and inspire. Your relationship will reflect your heart's most sacred light.

18.

Expressing Pleasure and Hurt

❦

When I am with you, I want to know how I'm affecting you. I really want to know how you are feeling, right now, in the present moment. I want to know what your deepest heart is feeling. But often, I am dumbfounded by your emotional responses. Everything seems fine to me, and then suddenly you are angry, or crying, or upset about something.

When we talk about it, I often discover that your emotions started with something that I did yesterday, or ten minutes ago. So, I'm frustrated. You are upset, but I can't do anything about the past, and I often don't remember things as you do. Sometimes you can't tell me why you feel so bad. And I don't seem very good at figuring it out, especially when you don't exactly know yourself.

But there are other times when your emotional responses open my heart. When I do something that hurts you and you immediately show me your hurt, then I can understand your feelings. My heart can feel your heart's response to my actions, right now. I really treasure when you immediately show me your pleasure or your pain, because then I can learn and grow. I truly do want to know how you are feeling, but I best learn how to be with you more deeply and with more integrity by knowing your feeling-response right now, as your deepest heart unfolds, not by hearing about what you have held in from the past.

Sexually and in everyday life, when your lover can feel your energy and skillfully guide you to deeper and more passionate flow, your body relaxes. You can trust him, and surrender to the depth of his loving command. When he seems unable to feel you, then you naturally withdraw your trust, take control, and do your best to lead yourself.

It's sexy to receive your man's love-capacity feeling and moving with your energy, taking you to more thrilling highs of pleasure and profound depths of surrender; just so, he finds your energetic responsiveness to be sexy. In fact, most men find nothing sexier than a woman's responsiveness.

In sexual embrace with your trusted lover, does your entire body ripple open when his fingertip grazes your nipple? Do you openly weep when he offers you his love? Does your heart respond in devotional worship when he offers you his deep consciousness and presence?

Few men are worthy of your total trust, but if you *were* with a trustable man would you be able to offer your body wide open, surrendering open beyond the edges of the universe, offering him more of your awesome pleasure than he has ever had the blessing to behold?

You will attract and inspire a man who can take you open into bliss as deeply as you can offer him your heart's bliss to take through the love-responsiveness of your body. The greatest asset of sexiness you can offer a deep man is your heart's energy rippling out through your body, through the way you move your hips, show your breasts, moan your pleasure, and writhe your surrender.

A young rigid woman, closed down and energetically dead, is far less sexy than an older woman who offers her heart-open pleasure in surges of abandoned moans and undulating sensuality, whose devotional eyes and mouth and vagina and legs move and open as unquenchable yearning, whose trust is total, who gives her man her deepest heart and every ounce of her own pleasure as a gift for him to feel, worship, and behold—such a woman is agelessly sexy. She is grounded in her heart and generous with love's offering.

Besides your heart's pleasure, your heart's pain is also a gift, if given through an open body and heart. You can imagine what it feels like to be with your man as he looks deep into your eyes, sits tall and strong, feels into your heart, and without averting his gaze, he begins crying. Feeling a man so vulnerable in his strength is incredibly sexy. Likewise, when you allow your emotions to be seen and felt fully through your body, face, and sound, your man feels your responsive aliveness and yearning, your openness to be moved by love's energy.

But there is a big difference between *accumulating* your emotions—eventually expressing them in a toxic dump of tense build-up—and being able to *spontaneously express* every nuance of emotion as the flow opens through you. Spontaneous emotional expression, from your deep heart through your open body and relaxed breath with no closure or tension, is a natural expression of love—even if love is expressed as sorrow, anger, or fear.

With practice, you can learn to offer your pleasure, pain, and emotions spontaneously and *responsively* as soon as they occur, letting go of them instantly, always with your heart open and connecting with your lover's heart, even as your pleasure, pain, and emotions flow. The moment you close your eyes, tense your belly or jaw, turn away, restrain your breath, or collapse in a ball on the floor, you are no longer opening but closing. Emotional flow now becomes pent-up energy, and sharing this accumulated, undigested emotional mass with your lover doesn't allow him to feel your heart's open yearning.

A weeping and open woman is very sexy; a weeping and closed woman is not.

You can learn to stay open while all of your emotions flow. Even when anger is flowing, you can learn to remain in eye contact with your lover. You can practice breathing with him, feeling his heart, feeling his love for you and your love for him. You can practice relaxing your body open, offering him your vulnerable heart's pain and yearning even while you are yelling and shouting.

All emotions can and do flow when your heart is open and connected with your lover's heart. This openness is sexy, even if it is also angry, or sad, or afraid. You simply offer your emotions through the openness of your body and heart as they ripple through you. No residue remains. You may scream in rage one moment and then open to be taken sexually in the next moment.

With practice, you can express your emotions from your deepest heart through your open body in spontaneous response to everything, both seen and unseen. Like the weather, your emotions are too huge and complex, their influences too numerous and untraceable, to be mentally understandable. You don't have to know *why* you feel whatever you are feeling in order to open and express your heart's deep yearning.

A key to deepening intimacy is to keep your heart's yearning open and connected with your lover while your emotions move through you. If you are afraid to express yourself, then you will accumulate pent-up emotions inside.

For instance, if your man is not fully present with you, then your heart will feel hurt. If you don't allow this hurt to be expressed fully and spontaneously from your open heart—as tears or cries of pain—then this emotional energy becomes frustrated behind your suppression and transforms into anger. Your *primary emotion,* in this case, is hurt. Your *secondary emotion* is anger, built by the suppression of your hurt.

You can let loose the secondary emotion—anger—for your own sake, just to release tension and let go of stress. You can shout and bang on a pillow, for instance. But your man will find your secondary emotion unworkable and not particularly inviting. To him, your secondary emotional energy will feel like vestigial tension from the past. And your primary emotion—hurt, in this case—will remain unexpressed. Your man won't be able to feel your heart's genuine yearning.

One key to cultivating a deep relationship is to always express your deepest yearning through the primary emotion that emerges from your open heart. Express your deepest heart immediately and spontaneously through your open and relaxed body, before suppressing it and allowing a secondary emotion to build up inside.

Offer your man the spontaneous and responsive music of your yearning heart, which is expressed through your primary emotion. Your primary emotion may be anger, hurt, sadness, fear, grief, or any energy emerging from your heart's deepest longing. Old hurts may also flush out, but everything is offered from the deepest place of love's yearning that you can occupy.

How will your man respond to the spontaneous expression of your heart's primary emotion? Lesser men will try to silence you through domination or try to calm you down so you can talk about your feelings. But a deep man will fully inhabit your heart's music. His deep inhabitance will serve to open your heart, and your primary emotion will express fully with no residue.

Give yourself and your man some time to change gears from your old ways of relating. Give your man a chance to learn how to open with your deeper heart's expression. It takes practice and courage to risk opening your hearts together as your primary emotions flow.

When your heart's yearning is open and connected with your lover's heart, you may scream and then relax and laugh. You may cry and then smile, feeling your man's loving presence. Your primary emotions will continue to cycle and flow, but you won't suppress yourself even for a moment, and so no secondary emotions will have a chance to build up inside of you.

You won't find yourself "needing to talk about something" with your man too often, because moment by moment your heart is expressing everything, while also yearning more deeply open in response to being claimed. Knowing you won't have to explain your feelings allows you to relax in deeper and fuller expression.

Your claimed heart is unafraid to offer your spontaneous emotional music. You do not fear loss of love or disapproval, nor do you think that you are weak for enjoying your man's claim of your heart. Your heart is inhabited by your man's unflinching presence, and therefore your heart can spontaneously sing or wail or weep—while opening in devotion to the love that fills you so fully.

19.

Masculine
Insensitivity

◦〜

I look at you sometimes and wonder, "What is going on with her?" I can tell that something is happening, but I don't know what. Are you angry but not showing it? Are you bored but not saying it? Are you simply happy and relaxed? Sometimes I really can't tell.

Even during sex I wonder. Are you motionless because you are lost in bliss or because you are trying to give me a message that you are tired? Did you just have an orgasm or did I accidentally hurt you, so you trembled and moaned? Are you ready to stop making love or just getting started?

I try to feel into you but often I'm at a loss. Your women friends don't seem to have this problem. They seem able to read your feelings in

the subtle way you narrow your eyes or pause as
you speak or withhold your touch. But I'm not as
sensitive as your friends are, although I really do
want to get your messages. I need you to amplify
your communication for my sake so I can notice
and hopefully understand the messages you
may be sending.

The masculine lives in a domain of goals and schedules, righteousness and injustice, success and failure. He probably can't feel the subtle energetic messages that you give him until your energy is quite loud. You might be angry for three days before he notices and asks, "Is something wrong?" Likewise, in bed, your pleasure may be invisible to him as he wonders, "Did you come?"

The masculine is not sensitive to the very energy that is your most obvious environment. Therefore, you may need to exaggerate your responses if you want your man to take your heart into account. Don't fake your feelings. Fully embody and exaggeratedly magnify your heart's true response for the sake of your man's "deafness" and "blindness" compared to your sensitivity.

When your heart is thrilled with the depth and integrity your man is offering, then show him. Loudly. Overtly. Wrap yourself around him as you make orgasmic sounds of pleasure. Tell him that you worship his integrity. Actually say, "I worship the depth of your consciousness. I worship your depth of heart. I love your integrity."

On the other hand, when your man is off, when his integrity disintegrates behind his false pursuits and narrow blindness, let him know equally loudly. Yell and scream. Weep and tremble. Show your disgust as if acting on a stage to an audience of thousands. Magnify your displeasure as well as your pleasure, and your man will notice.

Although lesser men will run or turn away—you'd be better off without them anyway—a deep man will respond to your worship or wrath with instantaneous correction of action. Your worship of his integrity draws him deeper into love, opening him to feel deep into your heart's intuition and wisdom, encouraging him and empowering his commitment to love's depth. Your wrath in response to his occasional self-deception or numb ambiguity will be a slap on his face, awakening him to an emergency situation of which he was probably unaware, giving him the opportunity to take urgent measures instead of blindly bumbling on.

Without your exaggerated heart-responsiveness, your man will tend to lose touch with everything but his own agenda. He may be able to maintain a relationship with you, but his consciousness tends to become shallowed in the pursuit of paths and points of completion. His life becomes flat. Your heart's fully offered energy—wrathful or devotional—awakens and deepens your man's heart into a domain of otherwise inaccessible sensitivity.

Remember that your heart's expressions don't always need to be squeezed into words of sensible reason. Sometimes it is better to give your man a chance to feel your heart-responsive energy without trying to mentally figure out the content through your words. You may not be able to exactly explain your feelings, anyway. You may want to give him a chance to feel and penetrate your flow with his loving presence so he can come to know your deepest heart as his. Then, even your heart's inexplicable and unfathomable wisdom can fine-tune his life's offering—as long as you magnify your responses enough so he notices!

20.

How to
Stay Open

You and I have habits that act to separate us, especially in times of intensity. When we are upset with each other, sometimes I get terse and rigid. Sometimes you appear to get swept away in the flow of your emotions, and I can no longer feel your heart of love. I know you love me. And I love you. But sometimes we get lost inside our own shells of closure, and we don't allow our hearts to connect in love.

I want to learn how to stay deeply connected with you in love, even when our shells of fear would otherwise keep us apart. I commit to practicing love, first by loving myself as I am right now, and then by loving you as you are right now. But beyond that, I commit to opening as the love that lives larger than you or me *or our relationship. I want to join with you in two-bodied loving so we can learn to open as the love that lives as the entire universe, the love yearning open from the depths of everyone's heart.*

Some women confuse openness with a sense of feeling good. But you can be open and still feel great pain or the full range of emotional music. You can be angry, sad, or even afraid and still be open. You can want to kill your man and still be open. Openness is a trust of what you are feeling—this trust is love. Whatever you feel, you can love your own emotions as well as your man's—and beyond.

With practice, your heart trusts open, loving your shells, your emotions, and whatever energy moves through you and your man, no matter how bad you feel. When you can open in trust then you are alive as love, even when love flows as the energy of anger, sadness, or fear. To allow you and your man to grow into deeper love and trust, you can randomly practice five key exercises daily, especially during emotionally intense moments:

1. CONNECT THROUGH YOUR EYES

Suppose that your lover insults you, then ignores you. You are hurt and begin to fume inside. He looks away from you, or you close your eyes.

Instead, maintain eye contact. Even if you are upset, look directly into your man's eyes. If you look deeply enough into his heart, you will feel the part of him that you love, even if you are in a moment of hate.

Actually look into your man's eyes and feel his deep strength, integrity, and his love for you. Perhaps you can only see a speck of his strength and integrity amidst a whole lot of muck, but keep feeling into this speck. Do your best to love the muck, and then love deeper into his heart, feeling his love for you, even if most of him seems repulsed. He has chosen you; he is with you; deep down you can feel where he still loves you, right now. Gaze into his deepest heart, and offer him your deepest heart through your open eyes.

2. BREATHE TOGETHER

When you constrict your breath then you block your emotional energy. If you breathe fully, then your energy can flow fully. If you can feel your man's energy *while* you breathe fully, then his energy can flow fully *with* you. If you contract your breath, then you won't be able to feel your man or yourself fully. Your heart will remain isolated behind your suppressed breath.

So, offer the possibility of energetic connection by breathing open with your man. First, do your best to love you and your man just as you are, relaxing your breath more open. Then, feel your man's breath, matching your breath with his. Allow yourself to feel what your man is feeling, breathing how your man is breathing. Breathe together while gazing into each other's eyes, even if you both feel like strangling each other.

Practice to open your heart in love and trust by breathing your man in and out. Breathe his love and his stupidity, his strength and his blindness, his sweetness and his anger. Breathe all the qualities of your man in and out, and open so you can breathe *with* him as one breathing two-bodied being of love.

3. RELAX YOUR BODY

Relaxing doesn't mean going limp. To relax means to open so the currents of love and emotional energy can flow through your body unimpeded. You can relax and shout and jump up and down. You can relax and whimper and wail. When you relax, love eases your rigid muscles so that all energies can move freely through you.

Your softest parts are most important to open while you are flowing with emotion. Your lips and tongue, your throat, your heart, your whole belly, your genitals—all the soft parts in the center and front of your body are the main avenues—or roadblocks—to the flow of your energy.

If your belly is tight, then your anger will stay stuffed, only to erupt later in toxic release or self-abuse. If your heart is closed, your emotions will ricochet destructively, lashing inwardly or outwardly without love. If your jaw is clenched, then your head and body become disconnected, and energy will accumulate as tension in your shoulders and pound in your skull.

But if you love your body, if you open your belly, heart, and throat, if your face and genitals ease open and relax, then your emotions can flow freely through you. Your body can be moved by your heart's true yearning and the spontaneous flow of your deepest emotional energy—you will be danced by your heart's deepest love and energy.

Perhaps your dance will flow with grief or spite or terror. You can love whatever is flowing through you. If you do not clamp down and stop the flow, your energy will emerge from your deepest heart spontaneously, expressing your heart's open yearning, and then the next wave of yearning and energy will emerge through your body as love's free flow.

4. FEEL FROM YOUR DEEPEST HEART TO HIS

While gazing into your lover's eyes, breathing with him, and relaxing your body to be danced open by love's yearning and energy, also feel into your lover's heart. From your heart, extend your feelers into his heart. Reach into his heart from yours, and open your heart to receive his heart's love.

This is very difficult in the midst of emotional intensity. If your man is shouting at you, or you are hating your man, then your heart will try to disconnect from him to protect itself. You must intentionally extend your heart-feelers into your lover's heart in moments like these. Intense emotion is no excuse for a disconnected heart. If you want deep intimacy, you must practice connecting your deep heart directly to his, even when feeling his heart is the last thing you want to do.

These are the most critical moments: when you are hurting each other, will you practice loving your hurt, loving his hurt, and softening open so you can offer your heart even more deeply, feeling into his *deepest* heart while opening to receive his heart-feelers?

If you cannot practice feeling his deepest heart from yours, then you are practicing some degree of separation. You are denying the deepest yearning of your heart.

You are refusing to yearn open as the fullness of divine love—you are disabling even the possibility of deep connection with your lover. These are the moments when the most is gained from practicing to stay open.

No matter how callous or unpresent your man is being, practice loving and accepting yourself and your lover just as you are, feeling everything you are feeling, and then *open your heart to extend your feelers into his deepest heart.*

Feel your lover's deepest heart from yours. You can do this while shouting and screaming. You can do this while breaking dishes on the floor or crying your eyes out. No matter how your energy flows or how he turns away, you can practice loving the waves of emotional energy that move through both of you while opening your heart to feel his.

5. EXPRESS YOURSELF SPONTANEOUSLY

While you maintain the previous practices—staying in eye contact, breathing together, relaxing your body open, and feeling your lover's deepest heart from yours—you can practice trusting the spontaneous emotional expression emerging from your heart. Just allow your body to do what it does, as long as you are lovingly relaxing open and maintaining feeling-contact with your lover through eyes, breath, and heart.

Allow your body to be danced by the full and untamed flow of your emotional force and your heart's tender yearning. If anger moves through you, then love your anger, vulnerably allowing every part of you to move with anger—your toes and fingers, your belly and vagina, your legs and ears—while staying feelingly connected with your lover.

If you want, you can use words to express the flow of energy that moves through you. But often, your yearning heart is most fully expressed through whole-body, non-verbal offerings. Open as anger and show your hurt through sounds, facial expressions, and whole-body gestures. Allow your body to be spontaneously danced by love's deepest energy.

By learning to stay open with your lover, even while he is rejecting you and you are ready to tear his head off, your hearts are available to touch, serving each other to open in deeper expression and communion. His heart's persistent loving pervades your drama of opening and closing. Your heart's devotion provides an ever-welcoming home for your man's fearful coming and going.

Over time, all excuses to stay closed evaporate in love's openness. Then, you can truly extend your heart's yearning beyond self-love, through the two-bodied form of devotional openness, and to all beings, without your shells—or his—holding you back.

By learning to love your shells and your lover's, and then loving through your shells to connect fully with your lover's deepest heart, you begin to learn how to feel the deepest heart of all beings, breathing the joy and suffering of all beings, opening as the love that lives and yearns at everyone's heart.

21.

Opening Beyond
an Impasse

I have learned more from you about my own blindness than from anyone else. Many times, your pained face and wounded heart have shown me that I have been living short of my potential, offering my life with less integrity than my heart could truly offer. I just can't see it by myself.

I try. I'm willing to look at my life and listen to the feedback of others. But even so, I have blind spots that apparently allow me to continue living in ways that are less true to love than I can live. And your heart's sensitivity always shows me what I can't see because of my own shells. I trust your heart's depth to reveal the parts of my life that my shells keep hidden from my view.

Because the feminine is connected with the flow of life energy much more intimately than the masculine is, you will often feel when your man is "off" before he does. You will be able to feel instantly when he is lying to himself or to others. Your heart will cringe. Your body will tense. Your breath will tighten.

You may not know exactly why. You may not be able to precisely articulate what you feel is "off" about your man's actions; you just know that your heart feels something is amiss. Your man is not living his deepest truth, he is not feeling your heart and everybody else's as deeply as he can: he is deceiving himself, living in his own justifications, and choosing a course that is less than his deepest gift.

You may try to tell him about what you feel, but he can't see it. Or, he may admit that he is "off," and then he may do nothing about it. When you try to talk with him about the way he is living his life, you may feel him defending himself, getting angry and deflecting your insight.

He may tell you that you are projecting your own needs onto him. He may claim that he is being honest with himself and with you, or that he is doing everything he can. Eventually, you may just give up trying to help him see his blind spot. You may even begin to question your own heart—do you really feel his self-deception or is it your own block that you are up against? Are you the one who can't feel your man's integrity, or is his integrity actually "off"? Are you afraid to totally surrender to your man's sexual claim, or is he truly blind to your deepest heart's yearning?

If you don't trust your man, you can't surrender open with him, sexually or otherwise. If he denies that he is "off" but you continue to feel it, then your frustration, rage, and confusion build inside. You begin to feel stuck, full of pain, unable to tell what is "his stuff" or "your stuff." The separation between you and your man grows.

Naturally, you try to guide yourself when you don't fully trust your man. You begin to rely on your own masculine capacity to navigate, since your man seems unwilling to even consider that he has a blind spot limiting his integrity. Or, he considers it, feels nothing, and then dismisses it as your own emotional neediness and lack of trust. Yet, you can still feel something off, something not quite right, about the way your man is conducting himself in the world and in bed.

Other than those critical moments when telling your man exactly what to do is definitely called for, your two-bodied trust would grow deepest by giving your man your fully expressed feelings while allowing him the chance to correct his own actions. Rather than telling him exactly what to *do* with your masculine directional guidance, tell him with words and show him through your body and expressions how you *feel*.

Reflect to him how his "offness" hurts you and affects your heart. Rather than saying, "I think you should do such and such," express what you feel—hurt, anxious, mistrustful—but allow him to find his own way to a correction and learn to navigate from a deeper truth.

If you regularly tell your man what to do—even if you can clearly see what course he needs to take—then you are depriving him of a learning opportunity. You are stepping in and applying your masculine capacity to navigate rather than allowing him the chance to exercise and cultivate his own masculine navigational skills. You are creating a relationship in which he will come to depend on your masculine guidance. Is this what you want? Can you fully surrender your heart and body to a man who regularly depends on you to tell him what to do?

Obviously, there are critical moments in life when you should step in and take charge for the sake of you, your man, and your family. But how often do you want to be in charge of your man because he hasn't learned to navigate? How is your sexual desire for one another affected when you take charge and tell him what to do?

Learn to trust and value your heart's deep sensitivity. Fully express to your man how you feel as your lives proceed together, moment by moment. But, as frequently as it feels appropriate, give your man the opportunity to step into the space of being the navigator. If you don't relinquish this space for him to step into, then he may never learn to guide with integrity and correct his own errors, and you may never fully trust him with your heart's surrender, sexually or spiritually. Your man may be willing to listen to what you think he should do, but the price you pay for him stepping aside to let you navigate is sexual neutralization and spiritual mistrust.

Meanwhile, don't suppress your pain and passively wait for him to get his act together. Show him your wince every time his actions are shallower than you know he is capable of living. Shout your anger every time he persists in denying his lack of integrity. Every time you feel him unreceptive to someone's honest feedback—yours or his friends'—display your disgust. Give your man your fullest expression in response to his self-deception or blunders, and allow him the opportunity to learn how to correct himself.

Your energetic attunement is a gift to your man. He often gets lost in the surface results whereas you can feel whether his deepest heart lives through his actions. You can show him, through your pleasure or displeasure, how profoundly his heart-depth affects you. He probably has no idea that you are so pained when he lives his life less deeply than you know he can. He probably can't feel his own lack of depth—he gets lost in rote tasks and the results of his actions. Apparent success is often enough proof for him to think he is doing the right thing. So your heart's response may be his only way to feel that he could be living more deeply.

If you both stand within your shells, then you will remain at an impasse, separate and self-reliant. You won't be able to open in two-bodied devotional trust.

Your man may say, "I can tell if I'm living true to my own heart. How can you know this better than I?"

You may feel, "Why are you defending yourself? I love you and only want your deepest heart to come through your life and our relationship. Why can't you see that you are pushing me and others away, saying you are open to feedback but justifying somehow you are right? I can't trust that you will see your errors, so I can't totally give myself to you."

Your shells make you the last person able to feel whether your true heart is being expressed through your body to the world. That's why, as you grow more open in two-bodied love, you must choose and inspire a man whose spiritual and sexual direction you trust more than your own. And your man must choose and claim a woman—you—whose heart-responsiveness and deep sensitivity he trusts more than what he can see for himself.

22.

Ending Relationships and the Him-Shaped Void

I want to be with you only if your deepest heart trusts to open with mine. You and I both have fears and needs for security and comfort, but I don't want our lesser desires to limit what our deepest hearts want.

I want your deepest heart's yearning to connect with mine. I want our relationship to help open our hearts to God, which isn't possible unless we prioritize our deepest heart's yearning. If we aren't both committed to loving ourselves, each other, and all beings as deeply as possible, then our love will stop short where our fear settles for comfort and familiarity.

You have told me about how, in the past, you had stayed with a man who didn't love you enough to touch your deepest heart's yearning.

After you finally broke up with him, you still thought about him and even went back a few times hoping that things with him would be different, that this time it would work out. But even your friends knew it was a lost cause, and eventually you knew it too. You moved on, and now you are mine, dear lover.

I know your heart holds the shape of the man who has loved you most profoundly, and I want to love you so deep that your heart is shaped by divine love's yearning, opening wider than the entire universe.

As you practice opening your heart and body to flow with love's yearning, pleasure, and power, you will notice that fewer and fewer men are interesting to you. You find shallow men boring. As a lover, you require a man who challenges you with the fullness of his love and commitment, a man who claims your heart more deeply open than you usually open by yourself. Few men can meet your heart's requirements to be fully seen, deeply felt, and taken open to God.

If you are already with a man, as you grow, his usual diversions may cease to interest you. Your old habits of relating may continue, but your heart is untouched by his superficial contact. Perhaps you used to enjoy cuddling for hours; now you begin to want your man's deeper passion. You may interpret your desire in strictly sexual terms, but you may actually be feeling your heart's deeper yearning—to be claimed by God's force through a man's love.

Sex may certainly be a big part of it, but your genuine desire is for a man whose very presence claims you and calls you deeper. No matter how much resistance you put up, you want a man who can feel your deep heart—who smiles lovingly in the face of your surface refusal, gently embracing you, suddenly humoring you, thunderously surprising you, softly cracking your shell open, and entering you with such tender passion that you melt open in his love. His strength of love is unyielding and yet he always feels your heart.

There aren't a whole lot of men who can offer you this depth; there aren't a whole lot of women who can respond with equal devotional fullness. So, as you grow, you will find fewer men and women who understand you, and fewer potential lovers who you can trust fully.

But there *are* deep men out there. If you aren't attracting these men, then you aren't amongst the few women who are offering the irresistible devotion that would attract them. Look at your life: you are already getting, and have always gotten, the kind of man you deserve, equally committed to practicing openness as you are.

If you complain that you haven't met any men who can open you to God, or that all the good men are taken, you are copping out and settling for less from yourself. The depth of your heart's yearning offered through the pleasurable surrender of your body will always attract a man who can claim you equally deep—as well as attracting lesser men to whom you can say, "No, thank you."

If you haven't found a man worthy of your trust, or your current man doesn't seem able to meet your heart's desire to be claimed, then you haven't allowed your heart's yearning and body's energy to open through your moment-to-moment devotional surrender fully enough. You have been afraid, or mistrustful. You have held back. So you have probably ended up with a man who holds back—even if you have now grown ready to open more fully.

You may find yourself wondering if you should stay in your present relationship or start a new one.

Men tend to leave relationships too soon, always looking for a better option. Women tend to stay in relationships too long, always hoping that their man will change and grow.

To know whether you should stay in your current relationship, you need to know *why* you are in relationship to begin with. Your heart must feel its *deepest* desire in relationship, and then you can align all your decisions from your true depth.

For instance, is your deepest desire in relationship to raise a family? If it is, then stay with your man as long as he shares this desire with you—even if he is less than spectacular in bed and doesn't give you the depth of love that you want.

If your deepest desire in relationship is to create financial security and a comfortable home, then stay with your man as long as he co-creates your vision of life with you—even if your heart still yearns to be ravished open and your man seems uninterested in spiritual matters.

What do you feel when you feel into your deepest desire in relationship? You may want a large family, money in the bank, and a house in the country, but is this the totality of your heart's *deepest* yearning?

Perhaps, in addition to everything else, your deep heart yearns to be seen and known and loved so fully that your yearning unfolds wide as God and divine love opens boundlessly through you and the hearts of all beings. If this is a primary aspect of your *deepest* desire in relationship, then you want a man who evokes your devotional surrender with his undeniable love and undoubtable claim of your heart. If he does so, then stay with him. If he doesn't, then why are you choosing him to begin with?

In part, you may choose to be with your man for reasons of security and familiarity. You don't want to lose your cozy nest. If you leave your man, you may doubt that you'll be able to find another man who loves you more adequately. So, like many women do, you may stay in a relationship that doesn't touch your deepest heart.

You have probably stayed with a man who doesn't have the slightest clue of how badly your heart aches to be claimed. And even if your man does know of your heart's desire, he probably doesn't sufficiently offer you the depth, humor, and persistence necessary to tenderly penetrate your resistances, unfolding your deepest yearning through his love.

Your man has probably long ago lost touch with *his* heart's deepest desire—ask him the deepest purpose of his life and listen to his answer—and so he certainly doesn't know how to stay in touch with *your* deepest heart.

Should you stay or should you go? The best way to answer this question is to put a time limit on suffering the shallowness of your relationship. Are you willing to remain unclaimed by your man for another six months? If so, tell your closest women friends that in six months *they* should decide if you seem more deeply opened by your man's love, more deeply offered in your devotional openness, more deeply ravished. You may be the last person to know if you should stay or go. Your nesting instincts and fear of not finding another man may keep you with an inadequate man far longer than is healthy for your heart, hoping he will change.

If your closest women friends feel that after six months of waiting, for instance, it is time for you to leave the relationship, your heart will suffer. No matter how unravished you may feel, your man was able to offer you *some* amount of love. His penis entered your body, his care entered your heart, however shallow or uncommitted his entrance may have been. Your man opened your body and heart somewhat with his love, and this opening retains his shape.

Even after you leave your man, you will feel a "him-shaped void" in your heart and body. You will miss him, long for him, hope that he calls you and tells you it was all a mistake, that he can change, that he wants you back. Your him-shaped void yearns to be filled—by him.

This sense of longing for the man who was able to love you most deeply so far will last until another man loves you deeper. You will retain the him-shaped void for the rest of your life, unless you attract a man of deeper loving into your life. You may feel that you are weak for wanting a man who was clearly unable to love you as deeply as you wanted—a man who may even have outright rejected or betrayed you. You may feel that you are "sick" for wanting him so badly even years after your abusive or mediocre relationship has ended.

But you are not weak or sick. You are a woman whose heart naturally retains a void shaped by the man who was able to love you most deeply so far, even if that wasn't deep enough to stay with him. The only cure for your him-craving is to attract another man whose love opens you deeper than the him-shaped void that remains from a previous man. Eventually, as your devotional capacity to offer yourself grows, you will attract a man who opens you to God's shape through his loving.

Then, your heart will retain a God-shaped void in moments when you have separated yourself from divine love. Your yearning will be to feel infinity's claim of your heart, opening you without bounds, filling you with an abundance of presence and pleasure beyond your capacity to bear, forcing you open as full as all. Your heart will only settle for love's total command, and you will tolerate only a man who can offer you this divine and utter claim. His deep presence will ravish you open to infinity's bliss, taking you open in the He-She merger of God's two-bodied expression of love.

23.

Three Stages
of Loving

When you see a cute kitten or smiling baby, you light up with joy. When you hear your favorite music on the radio, you move with pleasure. I want you to be happy, but I also want your happiness to deepen. I want our relationship to be a way for our heart's deepest yearning to open as love's full offering with or without our surface happiness. And I know this deepening of love takes a commitment to practice opening, since sometimes we both tend to close.

To practice opening, we both must feel the subtle fluctuations of our heart's depth of yearning. Sometimes I'm happy to love you skin deep and luxuriate in your beautiful fragrance and softness, as if you were my love-kitten. Sometimes

I want to share more deeply by discussing our feelings and hearing about where you want to go in your life and our relationship.

But you and I can also offer our hearts to each other even deeper. We can feel our deepest yearning to be seen and known for who we truly are. The divine love that flows through our deepest hearts longs to worship and be worshipped. By noticing how deeply we are opening our hearts to worship, moment by moment, we can choose to share our deepest yearning even as we enjoy other pleasures of life.

Your man can worship the shape of your breasts. He can focus on your nipples, kissing you, nibbling you, forgetting all else. But eventually his narrow focus becomes boring. You want a man to adore your breasts, but you want much more than that. Ultimately, you want a man who loves your breasts but especially loves your heart—and beyond that, you want a man who loves your breasts and heart but whose life is given to God, who is feeling you and *through* you to the depth of this divine moment, not simply limiting his life to the pleasure of your body.

You want a man who lives his life as divine poetry, penetrating you with the deepest expression of his heart. He lives as if every moment were his last, so he always gives his deepest gift, to you and everyone, as if it were his final gift, his fullest offering of presence. Even when he caresses and kisses your breasts, you can feel his love deeper than your flesh, entering into your heart, and opening even deeper than your own heart. You can feel his love opening beyond all form, his presence opening you to infinity, to divine love without bounds, to God.

Stage by stage, your desire to be worshipped deepens. These stages develop through the years of your life as your heart's yearning grows deeper. You also fluctuate between these stages, moment by moment.

In a 1st stage moment, you want your body to be adored. "Notice me, and make me feel beautiful."

In a 2nd stage moment, you want to be physically attractive, but you also want your opinions and career to be valued. "I am a successful and intelligent woman. Listen to me, and value who I am as a whole person."

In a 3rd stage moment, you are ready to be worshiped as you are, as the light of love that lives as all life's power. "I am light. Take me, if you dare."

You are not just a body to be entered or a mind to be shared. You are the very light of life, alive as the love that yearns to open at the heart of all beings.

You are moved by a force of love much larger than clitoris and career. Your true power isn't limited by your body or created by your mind, but flows open as the force of love, alive and bright as the universe.

Your deep heart may yearn to be seen and worshipped as love's light, yet you may settle for a man who makes you feel needed for your body or mind. Although it may be painful to feel how you can ignore your heart's deepest yearning, your capacity to choose and inspire a deep man requires that you can feel the differences between 1st, 2nd, and 3rd stage moments of loving.

In a 1st stage moment, you degrade your heart's *deepest* desire in order to feel wanted and needed by a man. You disregard your heart's signals that your man is off the mark, that he is lying to himself and to you, because you are afraid to lose him. You suppress yourself so as not to frighten or offend your man, but your energy comes out in other ways, secretly punishing him back for not loving you like you want. You may settle for inciting your man's abusive anger, because at least his angry presence is better than no presence at all.

You may praise your man's strength so he feels good about himself. You may give up your needs to cater to his. Your heart wants to be seen and loved so badly that you will do just about anything in the hopes of getting and keeping your man's love. You don't trust yourself to take care of yourself, so you are desperate for a man to take care of you. This is 1st stage feminine neediness.

In a 2nd stage moment, you choose to set aside your heart's deepest desire in order to create a safe haven of independence and self-reliance. Even though your heart still yearns for a man's true love to open you to God, you put your intimate life "on the back burner" while you prioritize achieving your professional goals and taking care of yourself.

You may minimize the struggle with your heart's deep desire to be ravished in love by a man by avoiding the strong, penetrative power of deep masculine presence: either you live alone, or choose relationships with men who are so confused or safe that they give you the space to do whatever you want.

You want enough space in your life to exercise your own masculine direction, so you either repel truly masculine men or choose men whose masculine love doesn't have the clarity, depth, or staying power to penetrate your shells of resistance and enter your life, body, and heart too deeply.

Even after you have exercised your own masculine directionality to achieve your financial goals and established your life the way you want it, you may find it difficult to meet a good man. Very likely, you are more surely directed than most of the men you meet. Your masculine presentation—which has become a habit in your body, voice, and breath—attracts undirected men who are needy for your masculine guidance, rather than deeply purposed men of passionate integrity who would be attracted to enter your feminine body and heart with their full masculine commitment, presence, and respect.

Your unclaimed heart continues to wait, still holding back behind a masculine shell of directionality—alone or in relationship—and you begin to wonder if you will ever be *fully* met by a man and lovingly claimed at heart. You haven't found—or allowed in—a man who you would trust with your heart's deepest yearning.

In a 3rd stage moment, you know that however successful and self-sufficient you may be, your heart still yearns to be entered and taken open. You long to surrender all control and allow love to move through your body and heart, so you can be utterly *possessed* by love. Your yearning to give yourself as love grows stronger than your need for a man to take care of you or for you to take care of yourself.

You will only attract and inspire a man who is as deep as you are offering your yearning, right now. So it is very important for you to know, moment by moment, what kind of woman you are being.

As a 1st stage woman, you try to get your lover's attention by giving him love even when he is not interested. You become a "doormat" willing to put up with his disinterest because you hope that by giving him love you will, sooner or later, get his love in return. You know that deep down he loves you, he just doesn't realize it right now, so you willingly play the victim to his disinterest as you wait and try to attract him. You know that he has the potential to love you, he just doesn't know how.

As a 2nd stage woman, you grow tired of your lover's lack of commitment, his incapacity or unwillingness to claim your heart, so you stop trying. Your heart closes and your body armors its softest parts from the pain of possible rejection. You shelter your untouched heart in superficial shells of occupation: listening to music, pursuing a career, cleaning the house, talking with friends. You learn to create healthy boundaries, cultivate your masculine directionality, and trust yourself more, so you are not needy of a man's support. But your deepest heart still yearns.

Without a deep man to help you stay the course of love, your body can become chronically self-masculinized. You push yourself toward your goals, and whether you fail or succeed, your body remains unravished, unopened, and dry. You can try to emphasize self-love, directing your love back onto yourself in a curl of ingrown protection, but this is no way to be claimed open by divine love.

As a 3rd stage woman, you learn to open your boundaries and express your heart's deepest yearning in love's vulnerable communion. You learn to relax open as your heart yearns. You learn to trust love.

Trust love—not a man or yourself. No person is worthy of total trust. Any man will, at times, waver in his love or falter in his commitment. And you will often waver in your own capacity to love yourself, as you often have.

Only love—the love that yearns open at the heart of all beings, the divine love that lives open as this entire moment—is worthy of total trust. Rather than devoting yourself to a man or to yourself, you can trust, surrender, and be lived open *as love*. You can practice this opening as love when you are alone or through two-bodied devotional surrender. If you choose two-bodied practice, then it is important to feel how you may be using your man as an excuse to weaken or guard yourself.

In the 1st stage, you weaken yourself in the hope of getting your man's love in return for your acquiescence. In the 2nd stage, you guard yourself by holding your deepest love in check, hoping to immunize yourself against feeling too much pain. You can even become numb. In the 3rd stage, you give your man love even while he may be hurting you because *you are alive as love*, because to deny him your love is to deny opening as your heart's deepest yearning. You offer yourself as the immensity of love you actually are.

For love's sake—for God's sake, yearning open as divine love—you offer your body open as love's puppet, you offer yourself to be lived open as love's flow, you offer your breath, voice, gestures, and actions as love's fully given gifts.

Your heart may feel wounded—by your man's disinterest as well as by your own sense of being undesirable—and yet you can choose to open your heart and body as an offering. You can look into your lover's eyes and relax your body. You can soften your breath and open your feelers outward, actively radiating love from your heart while feeling his pain, his fear, his hidden love.

You may be sobbing. You may be screaming. You may be trembling. But you are not closing. Rather, in spite of the pain in your heart and the stress in your body, in spite of your man's staunch opposition to love or your own lack of self-worth, you practice opening. Love is your discipline, and it is not always easy.

First, you love yourself, even loving your shells and your closure. Then, tender as love, you practice loving beyond yourself. To counteract your tendency for self-enclosure, you offer your yearning open to your lover. You actively open your heart as love's yearning, breathing more deeply, relaxing your body through pain, resistance, and neediness so your heart can feel your lover's yearning heart completely—eventually breathing your heart open to feel everyone's yearning.

With practice, your moods continue to flow, but your love-tenderized body lives full as a perpetually active offering, your heart relaxing open to be claimed by the moment's (or your man's) deep presence, radiating your deepest gifts of love to all.

Living with your heart closed and your body tense attracts a man of equal fearfulness, a man unwilling to offer his presence unless you are pleasing him. Living open—even while your heart hurts—attracts a man of equal willingness to open and feel you in deep mutual worship.

24.

Love Is a
Living Art

 ℮

In the past, I have lain in bed with you at night, looking at you, touching you but getting no response, wondering why you seemed so distant. I'm feeling good, I'm very attracted to you, but you don't seem interested.

I've now come to understand that all day your body is being opened by my loving or closed by my lack of integrity, moment by moment. In fact, both of us bring the entire day's tension or openness to bed with us. Our bodies remember the dreadful wreck or glorious art that our loving has been all day.

You and I are committed to loving each other as deeply as possible. We are both committed to practicing the ever-deepening art of love. However, our ongoing practice of love constantly *fluctuates. The offering of our hearts together is deepened or shallowed by the choices we make moment by moment. I hope we can laugh together in our awful moments, learning through our mistakes, as we grow more skillful and spontaneously artful in our practice of loving.*

I magine you are in bed with your man who is embracing you, kissing you, his eyes moist with affection.

"I love you," he says, "I love you so much." He presses himself against you, ready to enter you.

You can feel his love. You can feel that he really means it. But you can't completely open to him.

Maybe you can't open because yesterday he said he'd clean the garage but has forgotten about it and never carries through with his promises. Maybe you can't open because while watching TV earlier he patted you on the back in a repetitive and mechanical way and your body carried the tension of his monotonous and flat demeanor. Maybe you can't open because he keeps talking about changing his career but continues at a job he hates because he's afraid to take the risk of living more deeply.

The love your man tries to offer you in bed takes place in the feeling-context of your entire relationship. If you are to trust him at night, then the intention of his integrity must be consistent—he must carry through with his promises and live the deepest life he can throughout the day.

Your body remembers. Every moment you feel him losing track of his commitments, getting distracted in superficial pursuits, deceiving or mollifying himself while continuing in a life that is less than his fullest gift, your body cringes and you lose trust. To surrender open in bed at night, your heart requires his deepest offering throughout the day—just as he requires the deepest offering of your heart.

While lovemaking, your man will be moved to offer you the same depth of presence that your heart's yearning has evoked and demanded all day. In bed, you will be moved to offer him the same depth of sexual surrender that he has commanded of your heart all day by his integrity and presence. The depth of your sexual merger at night is predisposed by the depth of your devotional offering and his claim of your heart all day.

You may have your own sexual blocks and emotional fears, but your surrender *also* requires *his* integrity. As a two-bodied form, *both* of you must be offered fully open, all day, to each other and the world. If your devotion *or* his direction is less deeply sourced than possible, then your sex will also be tethered to the shallows. In bed, your pleasures will be limited to stimulation and release, fun and games, a clitoral orgasm and an ejaculation, rather than utter love-ravishment—consistently—open to God.

However, all day and night, both you and your partner fluctuate in how deeply you offer your heart. Love is an art that is alive, and how deeply you practice your heart's art fluctuates moment by moment.

Throughout each and every day, you have 1st stage moments, when you are hurt or exhausted and refuse to open. Maybe you throw a tantrum, or lock yourself in your room and eat, or shut down in a mood, or swirl in a mishmash of thoughts. You have 2nd stage moments, when you merely want to talk with your lover about how your relationship is going but not open your heart to love's depth. Or you want to go to the movies and have dinner with another couple and keep things pleasantly social, rather than surrendering open in vulnerable whole-bodied devotional offering.

You also have 3rd stage moments, when you are *willing to practice* opening your heart and body to receive God's deepest claim, perhaps through a man's true love-desire for you. You are willing to learn to surrender your vulnerable heart wide open.

There is no such thing as a totally "3rd stage woman" or a totally "3rd stage relationship." Your relationship fluctuates through all the stages as you and your man open and close throughout the day, sometimes connecting with each other deeply, sometimes hiding behind walls of separation. A loving connection may sometimes happen by grace, but moment to moment you can *practice* if you want your art of loving to deepen. Love is who you *are* in truth, but *opening* as love can also be practiced to counteract the accumulated habits of contraction that may otherwise prevent the truth of your deepest love from being fully offered.

Although the depth of your love's expression may vary, your commitment and practice can remain singularly devoted. That is, you can *practice* the art of 3rd stage relationship and you can *practice* the art of being a 3rd stage woman, even though 1st and 2nd stage moments also come and go all day and night.

You can artfully recognize and open deeper than the coming and going of 1st and 2nd stage moments. Your man may have forgotten a promise he made, and so you shut down in response to his lack of carry-through. Instead of whining or making excuses, your man can admit his mistake, and with humor, panache, and directness, simply take care of business and follow through with his promise. This is a man you can trust. He simply acknowledges his failure, dusts himself off, and carries on, having learned from his mistakes. He continues to grow, learning how to be more consistent in his carry-through while deepening his living art of love.

The truth is, you are not hurt if your man is occasionally forgetful. You are hurt if your man consistently lies and lacks integrity—forgetting the depth of his love, withdrawing from you, and collapsing from infinity to a sulk—in the midst of inevitable failures and successes.

Likewise, you may occasionally swirl in the currents of your emotions and say something untrue and hurtful to your man. Instead of collapsing in moody closure and fortressing your heart in defense, you can choose to open your heart and offer your deepest yearning. You can open and *practice* 3rd stage love-gifting even when your habits want to close you.

As if you were a musician practicing your instrument over and over so you can play artfully, you can practice deepening love. You can practice love's art by looking into your lover's eyes a little deeper, feeling and breathing your lover's heart a little deeper, relaxing your body open to flow with pleasure a little deeper, all the while offering your feminine form and yearning as gifts of love. Your commitment to the 3rd stage art of devotional practice is what attracts and inspires a 3rd stage man of deep integrity.

Would you prefer to live less loving than is true of your deepest heart? How deeply are you willing to love yourself, your man, and the world? How devoted are you to surrendering open, right now, feeling and breathing love, practicing to live as love from your heart so your gifts can be given, most artfully, to everyone?

25.

Showing Your Heart's Light in Public

Before you and I learned to love so deeply, sometimes you would come home from work and seem particularly tense. When I wondered why, you would tell me that all day you had felt the "psychic sexual grabs" of men, and so you had to armor yourself. Your body had to shield itself, and I was feeling the residue of tension in your muscles and the protective closure around your heart.

Now that you and I can open each other so fully in our loving, you no longer suffer in the same way. You know how to keep your heart open, your body relaxed, and your energy unavailable for exploitation at work and in public. Some of your friends still engage in "subtle sex" or flirt-ing, and you understand their need. They want to exchange a little sexual energy with others, but not go all the way. So they practice halfway sexual co-mingling.

Through our full practice of loving open to God, you and I have now grown beyond the need to indulge in the random sexual barrage that takes place between strangers and even friends. You don't need to armor yourself against the "attack" of men's attention, because you are so full of love's energy you scare them away or evoke their respect. Most of your day, at work and in public, you have learned how to keep your heart's yearning open to God and your body's energy flowing full.

Now, when you and I come together, we may take a few moments to relax into our deepest hearts and practice feeling into each other's deepest yearning, but no armoring prevents our connection. After a few moments of breathing together, looking into each other's eyes, and feeling each other's hearts, our bodies are free to merge as deeply as we desire. Neither of us carries the protective armoring that we maintained before learning to breathe and feel the hearts of everyone, offering our entire lives from the openness of our deepest yearning, for the sake of all beings.

For now, imagine you are in a 3rd stage committed relationship with a man; the same principles apply whether you are in a relationship or not. You know your feminine energy is very powerful; you could attract a man to do anything, if you wanted to. So, as a 3rd stage woman, you wield this power from your deepest heart, for the sake of all beings.

For instance, when you dress and put on make-up and jewelry before going to work, you dress knowing that you are adorning your feminine radiance, joyously magnifying the gift of your love's light—but also you feel the effect you will have on others. You know yourself as a gift of love's light, an irresistible force of attraction. Your very form, the feminine shape of your body, the way you move and speak, can affect men so strongly they can fantasize about you for days.

Is this what you want? Feel what would be best for others in every situation, at home, at a party, or at work. You probably enjoy adorning your radiance. But feeling beyond your own enjoyment, whom would it serve if you were to attract someone's *sexual* attention, and when is it appropriate?

When your heart is fully claimed by divine love, you have no *personal* neediness to be seen. Your body is open and flowing, alive with sexual energy, radiant with delight, and resplendent with the shine of love—you don't want to desecrate love's fullness in the oinking barrage of men's psychic grabbing and groping. At work, for instance, you can circulate your energy fully in your body, but you know it would serve nobody to sexually hook men's attention.

Your energy remains full at work, and yet "hookless." Under your clothes, your genitals remain relaxed and flushed with energy, your breasts still pulsing with your man's worship. Your heart continues feeling outward, feeling all hearts and breathing your man, your children, your colleagues at work—breathing everyone's heart.

Your body is moved by the grace of love's flow, with no need to be seen for your own sake, no need to hook men's attention, and yet no need to *suppress* the power of your attractive force. You simply carry on with your tasks at hand and continue breathing, feeling, and opening as love's light, without needing men to notice you.

At some point during your workday, you notice that you have become stressed. Your head is tight, your jaw tense, your breath shallow. You have spent the day making major decisions for your business, leading meetings, and catching up on your to-do list. Somewhere along the line, you lost connection with your heart. You began operating on automatic pilot as a masculine machine of purpose. You accomplished a lot, but your body and heart now feel tight and blocked.

So you go to a nearby park or sequester yourself in your office. Perhaps all you have available to you is a stall in the women's restroom. Wherever you can be alone and unseen, you stand still for a moment and relax. You imagine your lover's belly and chest pressed against the front of your body. You breathe more fully, inhaling in and exhaling out of your heart, your belly, your genitals, your legs, and even your toes.

You begin moving, swaying your hips, raising your arms, and allowing love's energy to flow more fully through your body. You spend a few minutes opening yourself to be filled by the moment's presence, offering yourself to be claimed and taken open by the fullness of now's intensity. You dance open and alive, intentionally inhaling-receiving and exhaling-giving love through every breath, in and out of every cell of your body while feeling all hearts. Your masculine edges begin to melt as you lovingly relax and round out, abundantly flowing with feminine aliveness and juice.

Every few hours during the workday you do a similar exercise. Sometimes you open your heart and body more subtly during a meeting or while sitting in front of the computer. You know that however important your business is, if you lose touch with your heart's deepest yearning and your body's openness, then you are training your body to be unfeeling and tense. You are disconnecting from what is most important to you: love.

You know that you are as good as or better than any man at getting things done. You want to be successful and don't hesitate to achieve your goals with discipline and ferocity. But you do not reduce yourself to a functional machine of achievement.

You know that success is only worth achieving if love also flows fully in your heart, your body, and your life. So, just as you support your man to stay connected with his depth, you do whatever practices re-connect you with your deep heart's yearning and energetic flow during an otherwise stressful workday. Over time, you actually learn to breathe all beings in and out of your heart and dance love through your entire body during your day at work.

This process can take years to cultivate artfully, but soon you notice other people treating you differently. Men and women are very attracted to your openness and radiance, but also very respectful of your depth. As you value your own deepest heart's yearning and breathe the hearts of all others, you attract honor, respect, and even worship from everyone. They can feel the indestructible power of your loving and the vulnerable openness of your heart.

Your body is alive with life and juicy with sex. Yet, you have no personal neediness to hook attention from random men—you are fully worshipped in sex and love by your chosen man at home, or claimed by divine love in your practice alone.

If men at work flirt with you, you have no need to flirt back. You say hello and smile, but you don't hook into their energy. Your eye contact is short and sweet. You know that to spend excessive time looking into their eyes or hugging them hello would be a compromise of your heart's depth and your body's fullness.

Even alone in the restroom stall or sitting at your desk, you are able to open, receive, and be claimed so fully by the moment's divine presence that you almost always feel ravished; the men at work can begin to seem like cardboard robots of sexual need in comparison to the depth your heart requires. Your deep heart connects and breathes with their deep heart, but you have no need to entangle sexual energies or flirt.

You decide to meet some of your close women friends for lunch. As you walk into the restaurant you are aware of eyes turning toward you. You breathe fully, inhaling and exhaling the hearts of everyone in the restaurant. You feel their hearts, yet you do not energetically luxuriate in their attention. Your heart is open, your body relaxed, but your energy is not available for exploitation.

You understand that men constantly crave feminine energy, especially in safe forms that don't demand depth. A man will pay to sit anonymously in a strip joint and watch women dance. He is healed and enlivened by the liberally offered show of feminine pleasure and unbridled energy—especially if he lacks the show of feminine pleasure in his intimate life, either because he is single or his woman holds back her sexual devotion.

As you walk from the restaurant door to your seat, you can feel various men at different stages watching you. 1st stage men are most numerous, and they regard you as a piece of woman-meat to gobble, a potential sexual fantasy. Their worship of you is limited to their lust for your body. 2nd stage men check you out not only for your looks but also for your vibe. They want a certain degree of sophistication, elegance, and independence. They also lust for a woman's body, but they find a woman's mind equally, if not more, alluring. They worship you as a whole person and check you out for the possibility of being their "partner."

Perhaps there are also a few 3rd stage men in the restaurant. Like all men, they worship the feminine, so they look at you too. They see your shapely form and feel sexual attractiveness, just like 1st stage men. They appreciate your elegance and intelligent disposition, just like 2nd stage men. But they also feel through your body and mind to your heart's depth. They are turned on most fully by a heart of devotional depth surrendered to love.

A 3rd stage man worships the depth of your devotional yearning and the fullness of your feminine love-light. Your heart's openness and radiance may shine through your body, the way you move, the way you are dressed, and the eloquence of your voice. But a great looking woman who is smart does not fool a 3rd stage man. He knows death. His consciousness feels through the surface of appearances. He knows that all things, including your body and mind, are transient, passing, and brief. This entire world is always changing, and so he is rooted in deep consciousness, that which never changes.

From this place of eternal depth, he feels you. He can feel if you are needy of men's attention. If you are playing games. If you are acting independent on the outside but full of lonely fear in your heart. His body may enjoy looking at yours and his mind may appreciate your intelligence, but that is not enough to move his heart in worship. His heart, his depth, his consciousness, worships feminine devotional openness—a woman who loves to be claimed by God's ravishment, a woman confident in her light's attractiveness, a woman who offers herself as a radiant blessing through which consciousness can worship and be worshipped.

A 3rd stage man feels whether your heart is worshipping consciousness—which is his heart's depth—or whether you are distracted in food, talk, and appearance. His heart—his consciousness—bows in worship of your heart's deep yearning and utter trust of love's depth. Otherwise, if he doesn't feel your heart's devotional disposition, he returns to his lunch, perhaps enlivened by your physical and intellectual charms, but not moved to worship your depth or to claim your heart and inhabit your life—if you both happened to be available to an intimate relationship.

You arrive at your table, fully aware that you have been inspected by every 1st, 2nd, and 3rd stage man, who lusted for, appreciated, or worshipped you as a divine appearance of feminine love-radiance, depending on their depth and yours. And so have the women in the restaurant.

Every woman is checking out every other woman, gauging herself relative to the competition. 1st stage women compare body shape and youth. 2nd stage women compare success, independence, and intelligence. 3rd stage women recognize and worship all women as human forms of the feminine divine, just as 3rd stage men do. They feel the *depth* of your heart's radiance, or its lack.

So, while young 1st stage women don't find your older body too much of a threat, and 2nd stage women attempt to position you in their worth-knowing categories, 3rd stage women feel how fully your temporary form is an expression of deep love and light. Are your body and mind transparent to your heart's radiance and devotional yearning, showering the room with your gifts of blessing? Or are you afraid, self-conscious, or so wounded and confused that you have lost touch to some degree with your own heart's deepest desire and gifts?

3rd stage women move, feel, and breathe open as every being's heart—and so a 3rd stage woman can easily feel your heart's openness or closure. Your breasts may be more or less perky and your career more or less successful, but a 3rd stage woman can feel whether or not your heart is claimed by love and offered as your deepest gift to all beings.

So as you sit down with your women friends, each feels you depending on whether she is in a 1st, 2nd, or 3rd stage moment. As you relax in your seat, you feel each of your friends' hearts. You feel their suffering and their love. You breathe your friends' pain and joy in and out of your heart, permeable to their yearning and their agony. You relax your body open and offer your friends your love-energy through touching them, laughing with them, speaking with them.

Your voice and words are a song for opening their hearts. Your movements are a dance for bringing light into their lives. Your laughter is a rejoicing in communion with the women you love. The 1st stage part of you might notice a friend's new diamond engagement ring and feel jealous. The

2nd stage part of you might feel envious of her career taking off because of the new book she recently published and the big ranch she purchased. But the 3rd stage part of you—your deep heart—never loses touch with her deep heart.

Your jealousy comes and goes—you notice the cute waiter's ass and his beautiful hands, too—and still, your heart feels into everyone's heart, breathing in and receiving their love and their suffering, offering them your heart's worship of their depth, without entangling them in your envy or lust. You actively *practice* giving and receiving love from your heart's depth of openness, even though lesser and more superficial aspects of your body and mind are also vying for your attention and expression.

If you were single and available for a relationship, the 3rd stage men in the restaurant would notice your depth and strength of heart. Compared to the hurried, stressed, and self-worth-obsessed demeanor of most women, the confidence of your vulnerable and yearning heart shows through the openness of your body, eyes, and smile. And so does your untamed, undomesticated, unafraid energy.

A 3rd stage man would be able to feel that you are not afraid to destroy that which is less than love. If you were single, your eyes might say, "I'm available." Your heart-disposition might say, "I yearn to be worshipped and to give myself in devotion." But your energy also says, "And don't even try unless you are living true to your heart's deepest purpose, offering your heart's deepest integrity, and you are fearless enough to stay present with me—to ravish me—even when I am a wild slut or a crazed fiendess. Take me, if you dare. If you give me less than your true heart, I'll kill you."

A 3rd stage man would feel your demand for his depth of presence even while sitting in the restaurant from a distance, without talking with you or touching you. He would feel your heart's openness offered through your breath, voice, and motion, and he would feel your readiness to chop off his mediocre head should his consciousness remain shallow. He can feel you this way because you are offering devotion or chopping off his head right now, in the restaurant, simply through a momentary glance and exchange of brief eye contact.

He would also feel if you were not single. In relationship, your disposition would be one of unavailability to random exchanges of sexual energy. Your heart is already claimed by your man's deep worship, and a 3rd stage man in the restaurant would honor your heart's commitment to your chosen man. He may internally bow in recognition of your heart's deep offering—he may be silently awed by the blessing power of your radiant form—but he will keep his distance in respect. At heart, you and he are breathing as one—you and everyone are breathing one at heart—and so his 1st and 2nd stage desires open in transparency to the one heart of love that breathes as all beings.

During lunch, you are bombarded with various 1st and 2nd stage pulls, hooks, and jabs. A friend criticizes you, and another complains that you hurt her last week. A sleazy man walks to your table and tries to pick you up. The hunky waiter still entices you. Your food absorbs you, and you realize that your heart's love has been shallowed to the dessert melting in your mouth. Through all these moments, you do your best to practice opening your heart to feel and breathe everyone, relaxing your body open and offering your deepest heart through your entire being as a blessing of love's light to your friends and to all.

Your practice of heart-depth, love-offering, and exquisitely responsive energy is what attracts a deep man and inspires all beings to open in the trust of love.

26.

Choosing Abuse and Refusing Love

❧

I can love myself, love you, and offer my deepest love to everyone—or I can hold back. This is my choice. And this same choice is yours, dear lover.

You and I have practiced the art of loving together. We have gone to teachers and taken workshops to help us open and love. We have read books about how to open our hearts and awaken to the divine that lives us. You and I both know what to do and how to open so we can offer the gifts that flow from our deepest heart. The only question is, will we?

Imagine you had a friend who was in a 1st stage relationship: Her man controls her, diminishes her, perhaps even beats her. But then they make love, he apologizes, and they connect in deep intimacy. A few days—or hours—later, he abuses her again, only to be followed by tearful periods of making up, contrition, and then passionate lovemaking.

She comes to you for advice. To you, it is obvious: she should leave her abusive man. She, however, thinks that is too drastic. She feels her man might be able to change. That he really *wants* to change, he just can't help himself. He is willing to see a therapist. He really loves her. She knows it.

She tells you how good it feels when they make love, how passionately he takes her. You understand what she says, and may crave a passionate man yourself, but you can't understand why she would tolerate his abuse. You try to help her understand that she could be with a man who would offer her passionate love without the abuse. She knows that's possible, but the void in her heart is being filled by her abusive man, and she doesn't trust that another man could love her so deeply.

Her choice is to be an active victim of his abuse, offering herself to him to be pummeled and then loved, in cycles. This is her choice. It is not your choice.

Your choice is to wait for a good man. You are more comfortable in the 2nd stage, taking care of yourself while your career progresses, your friends grow, and your life improves. Perhaps you have a man in your life, but you know that a deeper intimacy is possible. Or, perhaps you are waiting man-less, dating now and then, having lunch with men friends, but nothing serious.

You are probably not aware that, like your friend, you are *choosing* to be a victim of abuse. This mistreatment is not from a man, but from yourself. You are actively closing, protecting your heart from love, shutting down so your body and heart don't ache so openly. You may be damaging yourself as much as any man could damage you.

Every moment that you breathe more shallowly than you would while you were deeply making love, you are actively training your body to feel less, your heart to open less, your love to flow less. You don't need a man's raised fist to diminish you; you are diminishing yourself. You are choosing to stay in a relationship with yourself that diminishes you, just as your 1st stage friend is choosing to stay with a man in such a relationship.

A man's threat and your lack of trust create the same effect in you: Your body tenses, your breath becomes shallow, your muscles contract, your heart cringes, and you become numb. You may cry, wondering if it will ever end, if love will ever finally embrace you and enter you? Will you ever be able to trust love, or will you always live in doubt and fear? Your feelings can become so walled-off you aren't even consciously aware of them any more.

A man's abuse or your own self-abuse can become so familiar it feels normal. You can become so used to living a tense and contracted life that you no longer feel you are actively *choosing* to tense and contract. Your choice has become habit. You doubt there is really an option. You are afraid to risk opening larger than your tense stance of self-protective control, just like your friend is afraid to leave the confines of her man's control.

You have merely shifted your mistrust from external to internal doubt. You doubt love, so you buffer your heart and harden your body. You can become afraid to leave the familiar lifestyle—and tension—that continually abuses your heart. You've grown used to some suffering, and you truly love your well appointed home, your friends, your cat, your garden—just like your girlfriend loves her man's passion. Yet, both of you are choosing to play the victim to less love than you know, deep down, you deserve.

Tonight you may feel fine. You had a great evening dancing with your friends, enjoying a fine dinner, seeing a good movie. Tomorrow you may feel desperate, alone, ugly, worthless, unable to get out of bed. Your cycles of emotional self-abuse resemble your girlfriend's cycles with her lover, being battered and making up, wanting to leave and wanting to stay—in any case, unwilling to open beyond the home of familiarity you have created, however inadequate the loving is.

Until you can feel the openness beyond your drama—he loves me, he loves me not; I'm fine by myself, but I long for a good man—your heart will remain tangled up in abuse. You will habitually choose your 1st stage dependence relationship or your 2nd stage separative independence, until your yearning for love breaks your heart open beyond the drama of love's coming and going.

You can continue to provide support for your girlfriend to leave her abusive man, but she won't leave until she is ready to stand on her own, away from the unending drama of being abused and passionately loved. Likewise, nobody can make you grow beyond your heart-protected independence until you are ready to trust love and yearn open without becoming entangled in the unending drama of aloneness and possible relationship.

Are you ready and willing to live devotionally open—feeling and loving the layers of deep hurt and pain as they peel away from your heart—and offer your deepest yearning even while a man's love and your self-love come and go?

At heart, beneath your habitually clenched shells, you *are* love. You can *choose* to surrender open as your heart's deepest yearning. You can breathe, speak, move, and live *as* love's yearning openness. But you may refuse to relax open because you are afraid to feel the immense pain still abiding in your vulnerable heart. Just as a financial or political challenge can give your man something to do with his life on the surface, an insufficiently loving relationship or mistrust of men may give you a drama to justify your refusal to open as your deepest heart's yearning.

How dramatic do you prefer the story of your refusal? Do you require a man to abuse and neglect you? Or have you grown beyond that need, so you are quite able to abuse and neglect your own heart's deepest yearning? If you are not opening as love's fullest yearning right now, then you are refusing—*because you want to*. You can blame your man or his lack; you can blame yourself or your lack. But right now, you have a choice: Are you closing in tension or opening as your heart's deepest yearning, breathing, feeling, and opening as the love at the heart of all beings?

27.

Wanting to
Be Opened

I love feeling your love. But also, I love feeling you open to my love.

We have practiced the art of loving consistently. Now that our hearts are connected in love so deeply, I enjoy feeling the play of your shyness and coy resistance. While you playfully refuse me or push me away, I can feel the certainty of love smiling deep in your heart. You know that I will come through your closure to claim your heart wide open. I enjoy feeling your resistance while I ravish you open—we both know you are already mine.

In the midst of life, you can easily forget your heart's deepest desire. If you have a feminine sexual essence, then your deepest desire is to fully open, receiving love's ravishment and offering your heart in devotion—to God, but most often, through a man. Your heart probably prefers the two-bodied form of devotion to the one-bodied form. You probably would rather be taken open to God by a man's love, full of deep passion and integrity, than take yourself open alone in a room.

So, your deepest desire is not only to open, but to *be opened*. That is, your pleasure is not only to feel yourself wide open, but to feel your resistances welcomed and inhabited by your man, penetrated by his love, and surrendered open as he enters your heart with the tender force of his love. Through your fighting, tussling, and refusing, you want to enjoy the pleasure of your man staying with you, entering you with love, humor, and persistence, and opening you to God.

You want to feel and trust your man's ability to open you, and the only way you can feel this is by refusing, closing, and resisting long enough to feel his capacity to persist in his loving. His capacity to persist in loving turns you on—not merely the fact that he loves you. You want to feel him loving you when you are being a total bitch, a screaming banshee, or a closed down ball of "No." You want to feel him open you to "Yes."

You cannot help but test his love. You may say, "Leave me alone," in order to feel him stay with you in the face of your refusal. You may criticize his weaknesses in order to feel him not collapse, but stay humorously present in the face of truth. This is what "ravishment" really means: that your man takes you open deeper than you are apparently willing to go. In your deep heart you want to open completely, but the drama you sometimes play is one of refusal and resistance.

In the 1st stage, you are lost in your moods of refusal and frustration. In the 2nd stage, you try to suppress your yearning, sadness, and anger, acting calm and civilized on the outside, going crazy with pain on the inside.

In the 3rd stage you realize that your feminine form plays the refusal of love in order to feel your man open you in spite of your resistance. Your feminine drama continues even in the 3rd stage, but it is played with humor, both you and your lover knowing that your deep hearts are one, even though you are saying "No" and he is opening you to "Yes."

In the 1st stage, you sometimes act "hard to get" in order to hook your man's desire. In the 2nd stage, you think acting hard to get is an immature form of manipulation, so you try to express your desires in a direct and civil way rather than going through the games of hide and seek. But in the 3rd stage, you realize that your feminine heart desires to feel your man *opening* you, in addition to simply being open.

Your 3rd stage man would be feeling you, loving you, right now, as you are. He would feel your deep heart's yearning to open in devotional surrender as well as your play of closure.

A deep man feels all of you as if he were "wearing" you like a perfectly fitting shawl of light. He "inhabits" you as water inhabits the shape of a cloud. He loves you and enters your form so completely, he *is* you, the same openness of love.

In a 3rd stage relationship, you can feel your man sensitively inhabiting you, even while you resist. You can feel him knowing you, perhaps more deeply than you know yourself. You naturally surrender to reveal yourself open in the pleasure of his inhabitance. You know yourself through his persistent recognition of who you really are, yearning open as love's fullness.

28.

A Summary of
Trusting and Opening

I trust your deepest heart, and you trust mine.
This trust is the heart of our relationship.

We both have shells that sometimes block
our loving and create temporary betrayal and
confusion. But through these times of hurt, we
have practiced to open, and we have learned
to trust each other's deep heart yearning that
re-awakens love's reign. We are committed to
the love that lives open at the heart of our lives,
the same love that yearns to open through the
hearts of everyone.

Your loving is an art that deepens as your life grows through phases. Sometimes your masculine directionality will step to the fore, perhaps when you decide to cultivate your career. Sometimes your feminine force of love-energy's hugeness will move you. Since you are composed of both masculine and feminine aspects, you will naturally demonstrate different parts of yourself at different times throughout your life.

But if you have a feminine sexual essence, you will yearn to be taken open to God by a man of deep integrity. Even if you are the president of a corporation and a great success in your life of endeavors, your feminine heart will still yearn to give itself entirely in devotional offering.

You may be waiting to be claimed and to offer all of your body and heart to a man you can trust to open you to God, even if you are a powerful politician with oodles of money. No matter how much masculine success or freedom you have achieved, if you have a feminine sexual essence, then your heart yearns to be claimed in two-bodied devotional trust, ravished and offered without hesitation.

In the world, in business, in politics, in art, let your love guide your actions. Trust what unfolds when you live from your deepest heart. Do what you love to do. But be careful that your love of politics or business isn't a disguised form of not trusting your man, or not trusting that a man can take your heart open to God. Be careful that your professional life is an expression of your deepest heart, not a substitute for being ravished so fully that every cell is entered and burst open in love's bliss.

If you are with a man that can't open you to God, sexually and spiritually, then you are choosing a situation that doesn't demand your total surrender. If you are afraid to surrender—if one or more of your masculine shells want to retain control of your life—then you will always choose a man who can't fully enter you, whose demand is weak enough for you to justify your own mistrust and heart closure.

When you are ready to surrender open and be claimed by love, you will attract and choose a man who can open you fully, a man who *does* demand your total surrender with the consistent force of his deep and loving presence.

Otherwise, if your shells still cover your deepest heart's devotion, you will attract and choose a man whose shells create blind spots of non-integrity, justifying your mistrust and sustaining your closure until you eventually forget what it feels like to be open. Your man experiences your shelled emotional buildup more than your deepest heart's offering, so he trusts *his* heart more and listens to *your* emotionality less. Both of you trust your own heart more than your lover's.

This is the basis of a 2nd stage relationship: self-trust, and the denial that your lover can know your heart deeper than you.

The 3rd stage is based on mutual worship of each other's heart-depth, recognizing that your shells make you the *last* person able to feel whether your heart is being offered fully. You trust your 3rd stage lover to be your heart's heart.

Your man trusts your heart to feel his heart more truly than he can through his own shells. He opens to receive your heart's devotional response to his integrity as well as your heart's cringe in response to his blindness. Thanks to your sensitive connection to his heart, your man can align his life more fully with his own heart-truth. He can offer you—and the world—his love and gifts from a deeper place in his heart.

Feeling your man's undefended and loving integrity, you grow to trust his steadfast commitment to true heart-depth—yours, his, and everyone's. You more consistently receive his trustable capacity to feel you and open you more fully than you can open yourself. You surrender open and offer yourself to him—shells and all—to feel, enter, and ravish open to ever-deeper love and blissful surrender.

You each grow beyond self-trust in the worship and trust of love larger than yourself. Your man trusts you can feel his heart—and his life's alignment to his heart's truth—better than he can. You trust that your man can feel your heart's deepest yearning through your shells, blooming open your deepest joy of surrender better than you can.

You learn to trust and worship each other's hearts as divine gifts that can open you more than you can open yourself, and as you breathe and relax and open more fully, you feel all hearts' openness, or love, as your natural responsibility.

29.

Goodbye

Our time together has come to an end, as every relationship does, sooner or later.

I love you.

Others willing to share their love with us have opened your heart and mine.

I pray that our shared love serves to open the hearts of others, many others.

Goodbye, dear lover.

R emember love.

Love yourself, your lover, and everyone, just as you are.

Practicing allowing your heart to yearn open.

Your active opening counteracts your habitual closure.

In your deepest heart, you and your lover yearn for something more than the passing enjoyments of work, sex, family, and friends.

Your heart is acutely sensitive to every moment that your man's depth is unoffered. And he is turned off every moment that your hardened shells nag and bash at his peace.

Beneath his dull face and your tension, love yearns to open.

Your yearning is a gift to each other and to everyone.

You can have everything and still be depressed, until you learn that you are here as an offering. You are not here to get; you are here to give.

You are born in human form, maturing through childhood, middle age, and death. No body or relationship lasts forever. Only your yearning—love's desire to open through you—is constant.

Your love is the same love that yearns to open at everybody's heart.

Constant yearning is the call to open and give yourself to all as love's offering.

You will attract and inspire a man as willing and able to open as you are. If your body is unwilling or unable to surrender open and fully express your heart's yearning and trust, then you will attract and inspire a man unwilling or unable to fully claim your heart open.

Your offering is a beacon; your man is, or will be, as deep as you are now offering the hole in your heart, your yearning to open as love.

Surrender open beyond the edges of the universe, and be claimed open by God.

Or, know that you are actively choosing less.

This moment is your opportunity to feel and breathe all, offering your dance of love and your heart of devotion as deeply as you have ever yearned.

David Deida Resources

BOOKS

The Way of the Superior Man

A Spiritual Guide to Mastering the Challenges of Women,
Work, and Sexual Desire

David Deida explores the most important issues in men's lives—from career and family to women and intimacy to love and sex—to offer the ultimate spiritual guide for men living a life of integrity, authenticity, and freedom.

ISBN: 978-1-59179-257-4 / U.S. $17.95

Finding God Through Sex

Awakening the One of Spirit Through the Two of Flesh

No matter how much we pray or meditate, it's not always easy to integrate sexual pleasure and spiritual depth. David Deida helps single men and women and couples of every orientation turn sex into an erotic act of deep devotional surrender.

ISBN: 978-1-59179-273-4 / U.S. $16.95

Blue Truth

A Spiritual Guide to Life & Death and Love & Sex

David Deida presents a treasury of skills and insights for uncovering and offering your true heart of purpose, passion, and unquenchable love.

ISBN: 978-1-59179-259-8 / U.S. $16.95

Wild Nights

Conversations with Mykonos about Passionate Love, Extraordinary Sex, and How to Open to God

Meet Mykonos—scurrilous madman and speaker of truth. A recollection of a unique relationship between a student and an extraordinary spiritual teacher.

ISBN: 978-1-59179-233-8 / U.S. $15.95

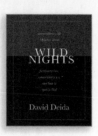

Instant Enlightenment

Fast, Deep, and Sexy

David Deida offers a wealth of priceless exercises and insights to bring "instant enlightenment" to the areas we need it most.

ISBN: 978-1-59179-560-5 / U.S. $12.95

The Enlightened Sex Manual

Sexual Skills for the Superior Lover

The secret to enlightenment and great sex is revealed to be one and the same in this groundbreaking manual for adventurous lovers. The ultimate collection of skills for opening to the physical, emotional, and spiritual rewards of intimate embrace.

ISBN: 978-1-59179-585-8 / U.S. $15.95

ALSO AVAILABLE (from HCI.com)

Intimate Communion

Awakening Your Sexual Essence

David Deida's first book lays the foundation for his teaching on the integration of intimacy and authentic spiritual practice.

It's a Guy Thing

An Owner's Manual for Women

David Deida answers over 150 of women's most asked questions about men and intimacy.

AUDIO

Enlightened Sex
Finding Freedom & Fullness Through Sexual Union
A complete six-CD program to learn the secrets to transforming lovemaking into a spiritual gift to yourself, your lover, and the world.
ISBN: 978-1-59179-083-9 / U.S. $69.95

The Way of the Superior Man:
The Teaching Sessions
Revolutionary Tools and Essential Exercises for Mastering the Challenges of Women, Work, and Sexual Desire
A spiritual guide for today's man in search of the secrets to success in career, purpose, and sexual intimacy—now available on four CDs in this original author expansion of and companion to the bestselling book.
ISBN: 978-1-59179-343-4 / U.S. $29.95

For information about all of David Deida's books and audio, visit **www.deida.info.**

To place an order or to receive a free catalog of wisdom teachings for the inner life, visit **www.soundstrue.com**, call toll-free **800-333-9185**, or write: The Sounds True Catalog, PO Box 8010, Boulder, CO 80306.

About the Author

&

Acknowledged as one of the most insightful and provocative teachers of our time, bestselling author David Deida continues to revolutionize the way that men and women grow spiritually and sexually. His books have been published in more than twenty languages. His workshops on a radically practical spirituality have been hailed as among the most original and authentic contributions to the field of self-development currently available.

For more information about David Deida's books, audio, video, and teaching schedule, please visit: **www.deida.info.**